CW01022709

GLOBE QUARTOS

THE WITCHES OF LANCASHIRE

RICHARD BROME and THOMAS HEYWOOD

First printed: London, 1634

This edition prepared by Gabriel Egan

GLOBE EDUCATION

and

NICK HERN BOOKS

LONDON

www.nickhernbooks.co.uk

GLOBE QUARTOS

This edition of *The Witches of Lancashire*
first published in Great Britain
as a paperback original in 2002
by Nick Hern Books Limited
14 Larden Road, London W3 7ST

in association with

Globe Education
Shakespeare's Globe, New Globe Walk
London SE1 9DT

Reprinted in 2008 (twice), 2009, 2011

Copyright in this edition © 2002
International Shakespeare Globe Centre Ltd

Typeset in Aldine-401 by the editor
Printed by CLE Print Limited, St Ives, Cambs PE27 3LE

A CIP catalogue record for this book is available from
the British Library

ISBN 978 1 85459 664 2

FSC
www.fsc.org
MIX
From responsible
sources
FSC® C019549

PREFACE

Over 400 plays written between 1567 and 1642 have survived in print. Few are now read and even fewer are performed. In 1995 Globe Education initiated a 30-year project to stage readings with professional casts of all the surviving texts so that audiences may once again hear plays by Barnes, Haughton, Shirley, Wilkins *et al.*

In 1997 Mark Rylance, Artistic Director of Shakespeare's Globe, included full productions of Beaumont and Fletcher's *The Maid's Tragedy* and Middleton's *A Chaste Maid in Cheapside* as part of the Globe Theatre's opening season. Over 30,000 people came to hear and see the two plays.

The popularity of the readings and the productions prompted Globe Education to approach Nick Hern to publish the texts being revived at the Globe to enable more people to read, study and, ideally, to produce them. Developments in computer typesetting have enabled editions to be published economically and quickly as *Globe Quartos*.

The first *Globe Quartos* were edited in 1998 by Nick de Somogyi. In 1999 an Editorial Board, composed of David Scott Kastan, Gordon McMullan and Richard Proudfoot, was established to oversee the series.

Globe Education is indebted to all those who have helped give new life to old plays: production teams, actors, audiences, directors, editors, publishers and readers.

Patrick Spottiswoode
Director, Globe Education

EDITORIAL BOARD'S PREFACE

The aim of the series is to make once more available English plays of the late sixteenth and early seventeenth centuries that have long been out of print in affordable form or have been available to readers only in scholarly editions in academic libraries. The *Globe Quartos* texts are based on the most reliable surviving forms of these plays (usually the first printed editions). These have been fully edited and modernized so as to make them easily usable by actors and readers today. Editorial correction and emendation are undertaken where required by the state of the original. Extra stage directions added by editors and needed to make the action clear are enclosed in square brackets. Apostrophes in verse speeches indicate elision of syllables and reflect the metrical pattern of the line. Prefatory matter includes notes from the director or co-ordinator of the production or reading of the play at the Globe and a brief factual introduction by the editor. Glossarial notes (keyed to the text by line numbers) explain difficult or obsolete usages and offer brief comment on other points of interest or obscurity. Departures from the wording of the original are recorded in textual notes that identify the source of corrections or editorial emendations. The opening page of the text in the original on which the edition is based is reproduced in reduced facsimile. Extra material relevant to the understanding of the play may occasionally be included in an Appendix.

ACKNOWLEDGEMENTS

The editor wishes to thank his postgraduate students on the Globe Education/King's College London MA 'Shakespearean Studies: Text and Playhouse' for their seminar discussions of this play. The early modern performance expertise of the Globe Education practitioners led by James Wallace brought the play to life in a staged reading that illuminated hitherto murky parts of it. Editing those parts afresh after the performance, I was glad to include a number of Wallace's suggestions. I am grateful to the British Library for permission to reprint the first text page of one of their two copies of the 1634 quarto. The *Globe Quartos* general editors, past and present, each helped with one or more of the problems I encountered. Most especially, David Scott Kastan and Gordon McMullan comprehensively mixed their labour with mine not only by advising on points of interpretation and editorial procedure, but also by indicating every occasion upon which I had failed to turn this seventeenth-century play script into proper modern English. What they missed, my student Alexandra London-Thompson caught. Having promised to absorb their lessons, I am grateful to be allowed pass off these people's improvements as my own.

This edition is dedicated to my wife, Joan Fitzpatrick.

Gabriel Egan

A NOTE ON THE STAGED READING

My first impression of this play was of an excuse for spectacle and amusement and little else. The witches are not particularly diabolical, as they are in *Macbeth*, nor is witchcraft placed in a social context of small-town poverty with its attendant prejudice and ignorance, as in *The Witch of Edmonton*. It neither frightened nor enlightened. That the real women involved were, at the time of writing, still suffering in jail for these supposed crimes seemed to add little urgency to the drama. Nathaniel Tomkyns's 'review' of an early performance at the Globe in 1634 appeared accurate enough: 'there be not in it . . . any poetical genius, or art, or language . . . or tenet of witches', but with its 'ribaldry', 'fopperies', and songs and dances, it is still a 'merry and excellent . . . play'.

The preparation for, and the experience of, rehearsal and performance of a staged reading revealed much more. The prologue's modest claim that a lack of foreign news was the occasion for a dramatization of domestic issues is disingenuous: Heywood was known for his domestic drama and, like his master Ben Jonson, Brome used realistic characters in contemporary local settings. Conscious art, not default, selected the dramatists' material. In all likelihood the labour was divided thus: Heywood wrote the spectacles of witch mischief and ancient village ritual, and Brome wrote about the inversion of social order in the Seely household, which is similar to the fun he had in *The Antipodes*. Brome's characteristic humour arising from character interplay is evident also in the subtly-executed scenes of the three young gallants. Whetstone is no caricature of a boasting fool but rather is fully developed, and the differing reactions to him from other characters and from the audience repay careful exploration. Master Generous too revealed more depth than expected. An audience is apt first to regard him as a pompous bore, but will become increasingly engaged with his struggle to think and act in accordance with God's law for the preservation of a Christian soul. The repentance of Mistress Generous is genuinely moving and her subsequent betrayal is all the more shocking for the effect she produced by her plausible act of contrition. The play is full of ideas about belief and disbelief, lies and truth, appearance and reality, and honest speaking and flattery. Over-credulity can spring from vice (the foolish Whetstone) or virtue (the good-hearted Generous).

Not witchcraft but witch-hunting is the play's serious matter. Doughty moves from scepticism to determination (his name suits both conditions) when frustrated in his lust for Moll Spencer, whose quarto name 'Mal' I kept for its connotation of maleficence. The play darkens with this witch-finder's zeal to see all the witches 'handsomely hanged', and we should credit the dramatists' observation of the psychosexual impulses underlying the witch-hunting craze.

Witchcraft shares with dramatic performance a concern for fortuitous timing, and our staged reading gained knife-edge immediacy by the presence, hot-foot from the Globe stage, of the First Witch from the Globe Theatre's 2001 season production of *Macbeth*. This provided an appropriate analogue to the link between the two King's men's plays which was clearly in the dramatists' conception of their work. The long theatrical tradition of bad luck associated with uttering the 'Scottish play' appears to have begun with *The Witches of Lancashire*: merely mentioning 'the Scottish wayward sisters' (as the quarto spelling has it) gives Winny Seely impaired vision and a 'hiccup' of the heart. Since they are all from Lancashire, the characters should logically all have northern accents, and I instructed the actors accordingly. The dramatists, however, chose to give only Lawrence and Parnell the necessary and nearly incomprehensible accents. Those wishing to reconstruct the early performances are referred for this detail to the 1634 quarto's difficult but amusing representation of dialect.

In performance it becomes clear that this is not simply an anti-witch play, since their victims suffer little physical harm. Millers were notoriously corrupt and here one is tied naked to his sails (on a very cold night) and another is pinched and scratched; such indignities scarcely exceed the likely fantasies of their customers. For these misdemeanours the witches suffer a variety of excesses from beating and amputation to arrest and threatened execution. In performance the final scene chilled those on stage and in the audience as the historical reality became immediate. Brome and Heywood explicitly name 'mercy' in their epilogue and throughout they present witchcraft unseriously while attending to the excessive response of state power. Perhaps this made a difference: unlike their unfortunate predecessors of 1612, there is no evidence that these Pendle witches were executed.

James Wallace

THE WITCHES OF LANCASHIRE

Cast of the staged reading co-ordinated by James Wallace at the Globe
Education Centre on 12 August 2001

Prologue	Liza Hayden
Arthur, a young gentleman	Nicholas Rowe
Tom Shakestone, a young gentleman	Tom Cornford
Bantam, a young gentleman	Dan Hawksford
Whetstone, nephew to Generous	Richard Lumsden
Generous, a wealthy squire	David Delve
Mistress Generous, Generous's wife and a witch	Beverley Klein
Robert, Generous's groom	Tony Bell
Mal Spencer, Robert's sweetheart and a witch	Lou Gish
Meg Johnson, a witch	Cherry Morris
Mawd Hargreave, a witch	Olivia MacDonald
Gillian Dickinson, a witch	Caroline Harris
Doughty	Michael Cronin
Seely, a wealthy squire whose household is bewitched	Robert Wilby
Gregory Seely, his son	James Wallace
Lawrence, his servant	Mike Rogers
Joan Seely, his wife	Virginia Denham
Winny Seely, his daughter	Karen Hayley
Parnell, his serving-woman	Sabina Netherclift
Soldier	Karl Stimpson
Miller	James Marsh
Boy, the Miller's son	Nicholas Kollgaard
Epilogue	Liza Hayden

*Spirits, Musicians, Country Rustics and Officers played by members of the
company*

On 16 August 1634 Nathaniel Tomkyns wrote a business letter to his acquaintance Sir Robert Phelips, and to lighten the tone at the end Tomkyns turned to some 'merriment' which he thought might interest Phelips. In London, he wrote, 'hath been lately a new comedy at the Globe called *The Witches of Lancashire*, acted by reason of the great concourse of people three days together'. For a repertory company like the King's men to perform a play three times in succession indicates enormous popularity, and Tomkyns explained that the subject matter was sensational: 'the slights and passages done or supposed to be done by these witches sent from thence hither', and moreover the supposed witches were 'still visible and in prison here'. Unlike most drama of the period, the play was about contemporary, indeed ongoing, events: the apprehension, conviction, and summoning to London for sentencing of four women from Pendle Forest in Lancashire found guilty of witchcraft at the Lancaster assizes. Tomkyns's 400-word eyewitness account of the Globe performance is reproduced in Appendix 1.

While the Lancashire women languished in jail in London in the summer of 1634, two seasoned dramatists, Thomas Heywood and Richard Brome, planned a play based on the case. Somehow they obtained transcripts of the witness's and defendants' depositions which were intended only for privy council use, and they drew upon these for journalistic details. One of these depositions, as published in 1677, is Appendix 2. When their play was nearly ready, the King's men successfully petitioned the lord chamberlain to prevent other companies performing witch plays, so preserving their 'scoop', and on 11, 12, or 13 August (we cannot be sure which), *The Witches of Lancashire* opened at the Globe.

In the autumn of 1634 a quarto of the play appeared under the title *The Late Lancashire Witches*, the word 'late' indicating that this was the recent story of Pendle witches, not a similar case originating from the same place in 1612. One of the British Library copies of this 1634 quarto, whose running header 'The Witches of Lancashire' confirms the play's proper title, is the control text for this edition. Brome and Heywood's play effectively takes the prosecution's side in the case, showing the women to be guilty of witchcraft and showing those who doubt this or worse, doubt the existence of witchcraft altogether, to be naïve. The most sustained bewitching of which they are guilty is the inversion of social order within the Seely household so that son and daughter (Gregory and Winny) bully their parents but are in turn bullied by their servants (Lawrence and Parnell). Although all the characters are from Lancashire, the dramatists chose to give only Lawrence and Parnell distinctive northern, provincial accents, represented in the quarto by inconsistent use of almost indecipherably non-standard spelling. It seems that a London audience could be expected to delight in regional stereotyping, at least among low class characters.

The Witches of Lancashire is the only surviving collaboration by Brome. Heywood had been writing plays for more than thirty years but Brome's rise was relatively recent, having had two hits in his first year writing for the stage, 1629: The Lovesick Maid and The Northern Lass, both for the King's men. To the partnership Heywood brought not only his extensive dramatic experience (he claimed to already have written or contributed to some 220 plays) but also his knowledge of witch-lore. The topsy-turvydom of the Seely household is an exploration of the comedy of inversion which Brome was to develop fully in his The Antipodes.

The play is highly comic but for a modern spectator or reader, knowledge of the serious predicament of the real subjects – most of whom denied the charges – can darken the atmosphere of its reception. Such qualms seem not to have troubled Tomkyns, for whom it was merely 'full of ribaldry', 'fopperies to provoke laughter', and 'diverse songs and dances', making in all a 'merry and excellent new play'. The historical record of the accused women fades into obscurity; although their accuser confessed to inventing his story, no pardon is recorded and the women were still in jail when they disappear from our view in 1637.

Tomkyns's end is better recorded: on 5 July 1643 he was hanged for counter-parliamentary treason.

Gabriel Egan

THE

WITCHES

OF

LANCASHIRE

DRAMATIS PERSONAE

The Persons in the Play

[PROLOGUE]
ARTHUR
SHAKESTONE } *three young gentlemen, and friends*
BANTAM
GENEROUS *a wealthy and generous squire*
MISTRESS GENEROUS *Generous's wife, and a witch*
WHETSTONE *her dimwitted young nephew*
ROBERT *Generous's groom*
MOLL *Spencer* *Robert's sweetheart, and a witch*
GILLIAN *Dickinson*
MAWD *Hargreave* } *three witches*
MEG *Johnson*
SEELY *a wealthy squire whose household is bewitched*
DOUGHTY *his friend*
JOAN *Seely's wife*
GREGORY *Seely's son*
WINNY *Seely's daughter*
LAWRENCE *Gregory's servant*
PARNELL *Winny's servant*
MILLER
BOY *the Miller's son*
SOLDIER
RABBLE *of hoydens*
Piper, Drummer, Demon-child, Constable, and Officers

3

[Enter] the PROLOGUE

Corrantoes failing, and no foot-post late
Possessing us with news of foreign state,
No accidents abroad worthy relation
Arriving here, we are forc'd from our own nation
To ground the scene that's now in agitation.
The project unto many here well known,
Those witches the fat jailer brought to town,
An argument so thin, persons so low,
Can neither yield much matter, nor great show.
Expect no more than can from such be rais'd,   10
So may the scene pass pardon'd, though not prais'd .   *[Exit]*

ACT 1, SCENE 1

Enter ARTHUR, SHAKESTONE, *and*
BANTAM, *as from hunting*

Arthur	Was ever sport of expectation
	Thus cross'd in th' height?
Shakestone	Tush, these are accidents
	All game is subject to.
Arthur	So you may call them
	Chances or crosses or what else you please,
	But for my part I'll hold them prodigies,
	As things transcending Nature.
Bantam	Oh, you speak this
	Because a hare hath cross'd you.
Arthur	A hare?
	A witch, or rather a devil, I think!
	For tell me, gentlemen, was't possible
	In such a fair course and no covert near,
	We in pursuit and she in constant view,
	Our eyes not wandering but all bent that way,
	The dogs in chase, she ready to be ceas'd,
	And at the instant, when I durst have laid
	My life to gage my dog had pinch'd her, then
	To vanish into nothing?
Shakestone	Somewhat strange,
	But not as you enforce it.
Arthur	Make it plain
	That I am in an error! Sure I am

10

	That I about me have no borrow'd eyes;	
	They are mine own and matches.	
Bantam	She might find	20
	Some muse as then not visible to us	
	And escape that way.	

Shakestone   Perhaps some fox had
Earth'd there, and though it be not common,
For I seldom have known or heard the like,
There squat herself, and so her 'scape appear
But natural which you proclaim a wonder.

Arthur Well, well, gentlemen,
Be you of your own faith, but what I see
And is to me apparent, being in sense,
My wits about me, no way toss'd or troubled,   30
To that will I give credit.

Bantam   Come, come, all men
Were never of one mind, nor I of yours.

Shakestone To leave this argument, are you resolv'd
Where we shall dine today?

Arthur   Yes, where we purpos'd.

Bantam That was with Master Generous.

Arthur   True, the same,
And where a loving welcome is presum'd,
Whose liberal table's never unprepar'd,
Nor he of guests unfurnish'd. Of his means,
There's none can bear it with a braver port
And keep his state unshaken. One who sells not 40
Nor covets he to purchase, holds his own
Without oppressing others, always press'd
To endear to him any known gentleman

	In whom he finds good parts.
Bantam	A character
	Not common in this age.
Arthur	I cannot wind him up
	Unto the least part of his noble worth;
	'Tis far above my strength.

Enter WHETSTONE

Shakestone	See who comes yonder:
	A fourth to make us a full mess of guests
	At Master Generous' table.
Arthur	Tush, let him pass.
	He is not worth our luring – a mere coxcomb. 50
	It is a way to call our wits in question
	To have him seen amongst us.
Bantam	He hath spied us;
	There is no way to evade him.
Arthur	That's my grief.
	A most notorious liar: out upon him!
Shakestone	Let's set the best face on't.
Whetstone	What, gentlemen? All mine old acquaintance? A whole triplicity of friends together? Nay then, 'tis three to one we shall not soon part company.
Shakestone	Sweet Master Whetstone!
Bantam	Dainty Master Whetstone! 60
Arthur	Delicate Master Whetstone!
Whetstone	You say right! Master Whetstone I have been,

Master Whetstone I am, and Master Whetstone I
shall be, and those that know me know withal
that I have not my name for nothing. I am he
whom all the brave blades of the country use to
whet their wits upon. Sweet Master Shakestone,
dainty Master Bantam, and dainty Master
Arthur! And how? And how? What, all lustick?
All froligozone? I know you are going to my   70
uncle's to dinner, and so am I too. What, shall we
all make one rendezvous there? You need not
doubt of your welcome.

Shakestone   No doubt at all, kind Master Whetstone, but we
have not seen you of late – you are grown a great
stranger amongst us. I desire sometimes to give
you a visit. I pray, where do you lie?

Whetstone   Where do I lie? Why, sometimes in one place and
then again in another – I love to shift lodgings but
most constantly. Wheresoever I dine or sup, there   80
do I lie!

Arthur   [aside] I never heard that word proceed from him
I durst call truth till now.

Whetstone   But wheresoever I lie, 'tis no matter for that – I
pray you say, and say truth, are not you three now
going to dinner to my uncle's?

Bantam   I think you are a witch, Master Whetstone.

Whetstone   How! A witch, gentlemen? I hope you do not
mean to abuse me, though at this time (if report
be true) there are too many of them here in our   90
country. But I am sure I look like no such ugly
creature.

Shakestone	It seems, then, you are of opinion that there are witches. For mine own part, I can hardly be induced to think there is any such kind of people.
Whetstone	No such kind of people? I pray you tell me gentlemen, did never any one of you know my mother?
Arthur	Why, was your mother a witch?
Whetstone	I do not say as witches go nowadays, for they for the most part are ugly old beldams, but she was a lusty young lass and, by her own report, by her beauty and fair looks bewitched my father.
Bantam	It seems then your mother was rather a young wanton wench than an old withered witch.
Whetstone	You say right, and know withal I come of two ancient families, for as I am a Whetstone by the mother side, so I am a By-blow by the father's.
Arthur	It appears then, by your discourse, that you came in at the window.
Whetstone	I would have you think I scorn, like my grandam's cat, to leap over the hatch.
Shakestone	[*To* ARTHUR] He hath confess'd himself to be a bastard.
Arthur	[*To* SHAKESTONE] And I believe't as a notorious truth.
Whetstone	Howsoever I was begot, here you see I am. And if my parents went to it without fear or wit, what can I help it?
Arthur	[*To* SHAKESTONE] Very probable, for as he was got without fear, so it is apparent he was born without wit.

100

110

120

Whetstone	Gentlemen, it seems you have some private business amongst yourselves which I am not willing to interrupt. I know not how the day goes with you, but for mine own part my stomach is now much upon twelve. You know what hour my uncle keeps, and I love ever to be set before the first grace. I am going before. Speak, shall I acquaint him with your coming after?	
Shakestone	We mean this day to see what fare he keeps.	
Whetstone	And you know it is his custom to fare well, and in that respect I think I may be his kinsman. And so farewell gentlemen. I'll be your forerunner to give him notice of your visit.	130
Bantam	And so entire us to you.	
Shakestone	Sweet Master Whetstone!	
Arthur	Kind Master By-blow!	
Whetstone	I see you are perfect both in my name and surname. I have been ever bound unto you, for which I will at this time be your *noverint* and give him notice that you *universi* will be with him *per praesentes*, and that I take to be presently.	140 *Exit*
Arthur	Farewell *As in praesenti*.	
Shakestone	It seems he's piece of a scholar.	
Arthur	What, because he hath read a little scrivener's Latin? He never proceeded farther in his Accidence than to *Mentiri non est meum* and that was such a hard lesson to learn that he stuck at *mentiri* and could never reach to *non est meum*. Since, a mere Ignaro and not worth	

	acknowledgement.	150
Bantam	Are these then the best parts he can boast of?	
Arthur	As you see him now, so shall you find him ever – all in one strain. There is one only thing which I wonder he left out.	
Shakestone	And what might that be?	
Arthur	Of the same affinity with rest: at every second word he is commonly boasting either of his aunt or his uncle.	

Enter GENEROUS

Bantam	You name him in good time; see where he comes.	
Generous	Gentlemen, welcome! 'Tis a word I use;	160
	From me expect no further compliment.	
	Nor do I name it often at one meeting;	
	Once spoke (to those that understand me best	
	And know I always purpose as I speak)	
	Hath ever yet sufficed, so let it you.	
	Nor do I love that common phrase of guests	
	As 'we make bold', or 'we are troublesome',	
	'We take you unprovided', and the like.	
	I know you understanding gentlemen	
	And, knowing me, cannot persuade yourselves	170
	With me you shall be troublesome or bold,	
	But still provided for my worthy friends	
	Amongst whom you are listed.	
Arthur	Noble sir,	
	You generously instruct us and to express	
	We can be your apt scholars – in a word	

We come to dine with you.

Generous   And, gentlemen,
Such plainness doth best please me. I had notice
Of so much by my kinsman, and, to show
How lovingly I took it, instantly
Rose from my chair to meet you at the gate   180
And be myself your usher. Nor shall you find,
Being set to meat, that I'll excuse your fare
Or say 'I am sorry it falls out so poor'
And 'had I known your coming we'd have had
Such things and such', nor blame my cook, to say
'This dish or that had not been sauc'd with care' –
Words fitting best a common hostess' mouth
When there's perhaps some just cause of dislike
But not the table of a gentleman;
Nor is it my wife's custom. In a word,   190
Take what you find and so.

Arthur   Sir, without flattery
You may be call'd the sole surviving son
Of long since banish'd hospitality.

Generous   In that you please me not. But, gentlemen,
I hope to be beholden unto you all,
Which if I prove I'll be a grateful debtor.
Bantam   Wherein, good sir?

Generous   I ever studied plainness
And truth withal.

Shakestone   I pray express yourself.

Generous   In few I shall.
I know this youth to whom my wife is aunt   200
Is, as you needs must find him, weak and shallow,

	Dull as his name and what for kindred sake	
	We note not, or at least are loath to see,	
	Is unto such well-knowing gentlemen	
	Most grossly visible. If for my sake	
	You will but seem to wink at these his wants,	
	At least at table before us his friends.	
	I shall receive it as a courtesy	
	Not soon to be forgot.	

Arthur   Presume it, sir.

Generous   Now when you please pray enter, gentlemen.   210

Arthur   Would these my friends prepare the way before.
              To be resolv'd of one thing before dinner
              Would something add unto mine appetite.
              [*To* BANTAM *and* SHAKESTONE] Shall I
              entreat you so much?

Bantam   Oh sir, you may command us.

                    Exit BANTAM *and* SHAKESTONE

Generous   I'th' meantime
              Prepare your stomachs with a bowl of sack;
              My cellar can afford it. Now, Master Arthur,
              Pray freely speak your thoughts.

Arthur   I come not, sir
              To press a promise from you – take't not so –   220
              Rather to prompt your memory in a motion
              Made to you not long since.

Generous   Was't not about
              A manor, the best part of your estate,
              Mortgag'd to one slips no advantages

	Which you would have redeem'd?
Arthur	True sir, the same.
Generous	And as I think, I promis'd at that time To become bound with you, or if the usurer (A base, yet the best, title I can give him) Perhaps should question that security To have the money ready. Was't not so? 230
Arthur	It was to that purpose we discoursed.
Generous	Provided – To have the writings in my custody. Else how should I secure mine own estate?
Arthur	To deny that I should appear to th' world Stupid and of no brain.
Generous	Your money's ready.
Arthur	And I remain a man oblig'd to you Beyond all utterance.
Generous	Make then your word good By speaking it no further, only this: It seems your uncle you trusted in so far Hath failed your expectation.
Arthur	Sir, he hath. 240 Not that he is unwilling or unable But at this time unfit to be solicited; For, to the country's wonder and my sorrow, He is much to be pitied.
Generous	Why, I entreat you?
Arthur	Because he's late become the sole discourse Of all the country, for, of a man respected For his discretion and known gravity,

	As master of a govern'd family,	
	The house – as if the ridge were fix'd below	
	And groundsills lifted up to make the roof –	250
	All now turn'd topsy-turvy.	

Generous   Strange! But how?

Arthur   In such a retrograde and preposterous way
                  As seldom hath been heard of – I think never.

Generous   Can you discourse the manner?

Arthur   The good man
                  In all obedience kneels unto his son;
                  He, with an austere brow, commands his father.
                  The wife presumes not in the daughter's sight
                  Without a prepar'd curtsy. The girl she
                  Expects it as a duty, chides her mother,
                  Who quakes and trembles at each word she speaks.   260
                  And, what's as strange, the maid she domineers
                  O'er her young mistress who is aw'd by her.
                  The son to whom the father creeps and bends
                  Stands in as much fear of the groom his man.
                  All in such rare disorder that, in some
                  As it breeds pity and in others wonder,
                  So in the most part laughter.

Generous   How think you might this come?

Arthur   'Tis thought by witchcraft.

Generous   They that think so dream,
                  For my belief is no such thing can be;   270
                  A madness you may call it. Dinner stays;
                  That done the best part of the afternoon
                  We'll spend about your business.   *Exeunt*

[1.2]   Scene II

Enter SEELY *and* DOUGHTY

Seely   Nay, but understand me, neighbour Doughty!

Doughty   Good Master Seely, I do understand you, and over
           and over understand you so much that I could
           e'en blush at your fondness. And had I a son to
           serve me so, I would conjure a devil out of him.

Seely   Alas, he is my child.

Doughty   No, you are his child to live in fear of him. Indeed
           they say old men become children again, but
           before I would become my child's child, and make
           my foot my head, I would stand upon my head   10
           and kick my heels at the skies.

Enter GREGORY

Seely   You do not know what an only son is. Oh see, he
           comes! Now if you can appease his anger toward
           me, you shall do an act of timely charity.

Doughty   It is an office that I am but weakly versed in, to
           plead to a son in the father's behalf. [*aside*] Bless
           me what looks the devilish young rascal frights the
           poor man withal!

Gregory   I wonder at your confidence and how you dare
           appear before me.   20

Doughty   [*aside*] A brave beginning!

Seely   Oh son, be patient.

Gregory   It is right reverend counsel; I thank you for it. I
           shall study patience, shall I, while you practice

	ways to beggar me, shall I?
Doughty	[*aside*] Very handsome!
Seely	If ever I transgress in the like again –
Gregory	I have taken your word too often, sir, and neither can nor will forbear you longer.
Doughty	What, not your father, Master Gregory?
Gregory	What's that to you, sir?
Doughty	Pray tell me then, sir, how many years has he to serve you?
Gregory	What, do you bring your spokesman now, your advocate? What fee goes out of my estate now for his oratory?
Doughty	Come, I must tell you, you forget yourself, And in this foul unnatural strife wherein You trample on your father, you are fall'n Below humanity. You're so beneath The title of a son you cannot claim To be a man, and let me tell you, were you mine, Thou shouldst not eat but on thy knees before me!
Seely	Oh, this is not the way! This is to raise impatience into fury. I do not seek his quiet for my ease: I can bear all his chidings and his threats And take them well, very exceeding well, And find they do me good on my own part – Indeed they do reclaim me from those errors That might impeach his fortunes – but I fear Th'unquiet strife within him hurts himself And wastes or weakens nature by the breach

30

40

50

	Of moderate sleep and diet; and I can No less than grieve to find my weaknesses To be the cause of his affliction And see the danger of his health and being.
Doughty	Alas poor man! [*To* GREGORY] Can you stand open-eyed Or dry-eyed either at this now in a father?
Gregory	Why, if it grieve you, you may look off on't. I have seen more than this twice twenty times, 60 And have as often been deceived by his Dissimulations. I can see nothing mended.
Doughty	He is a happy sire that has brought up his son to this!
Seely	All shall be mended. Son, content yourself. But this time forget but this last fault.
Gregory	Yes, for a new one tomorrow!
Doughty	Pray, Master Gregory, forget it. You see how submissive your poor penitent is. Forget it, forget it! Put it out o' your head; knock it out of 70 your brains. I protest, if my father, nay, if my father's dog should have said as much to me, I should have embraced him. What was the trespass? It could not be so heinous.
Gregory	Well, sir, you now shall be a judge for all your jeering. Was it a fatherly part, think you, having a son, to offer to enter in bonds for his nephew, so to endanger my estate to redeem his mortgage?
Seely	But I did it not, son!
Gregory	I know it very well, but your dotage had done it if 80 · my care had not prevented it.

Doughty	Is that the business? Why if he had done it, had he not been sufficiently secured in having the mortgage made over to himself?
Gregory	He does nothing but practice ways to undo himself and me. A very spendthrift, a prodigal sire, he was at the ale but t'other day and spent a fourpenny club.
Seely	'Tis gone and past, son.
Gregory	Can you hold your peace, sir? And not long ago at 90 the wine he spent his tester and two pence to the piper. That was brave was it not?
Seely	Truly, we were civilly merry, but I have left it.
Gregory	Your civility, have you not? For no longer ago than last holiday evening he gamed away eight double-ringed tokens on a rubbers at bowls with the curate and some of his idle companions.
Doughty	Fie! Master Gregory Seely, is this seemly in a son? You'll have a rod for the child your father shortly, I fear. 'Alas, did he make it cry?' 'Give me 100 a stroke and I'll beat him!' Bless me, they make me almost as mad as themselves.
Gregory	'Twere good you would meddle with your own matters, sir.
Seely	Son, son.
Gregory	Sir, sir, as I am not beholden to you for house or land – for it has stood in the name of my ancestry the Seelys above two hundred years – so will I look you leave all as you found it.

Enter LAWRENCE

Lawrence	What is the matter, can you tell?	110
Gregory	O Lawrence, welcome, thou wilt make all well, I am sure.	
Lawrence	Yea, which way, can you tell? But what the foul evil do you, here's such a din?	
Doughty	Art thou his man, fellow, ha, that talkest thus to him?	
Lawrence	Yea sir, and what ma' you o' that? He maintains me to rule him ,and I'll do't – or ma' the heart weary o' the womb of him.	
Doughty	[*aside*] This is quite upside down: the son controls the father and the man overcrows his master's coxcomb – sure they are all bewitched.	120
Gregory	'Twas but so, truly Lawrence. The peevish old man vexed me, for which I did my duty in telling him his own, and Master Doughty here maintains him against me.	
Lawrence	I forboden you to meddle with the old carl, and let me alone with him, yet you still be at him. He served you but well to baste ye for't, an he were strong enough, but an I fall foul with ye, and I swaddle ye not savourly, may my guts brast.	130
Seely	Prithee, good Lawrence, be gentle and do not fright thy master so.	
Lawrence	Yea, at your command anon!	
Doughty	Enough, good Lawrence; you have said enough.	

Lawrence	How trow you that? A fine world when a man cannot be quiet at home for busy-brained neighbours.
Doughty	[*aside*] I know not what to say to anything here; this cannot be but witchcraft. 140

Enter JOAN *and* WINNY

Winny	I cannot endure it nor I will not endure it!
Doughty	[*aside*] Hey day! The daughter upon the mother, too!
Winny	One of us two – choose you which – must leave the house. We are not to live together, I see that, but I will know, if there be law in Lancashire for't, which is fit first to depart the house or the world, the mother or the daughter.
Joan	Daughter, I say –
Winny	Do you say the 'daughter'? For that word I say the 150 'mother'! Unless you can prove me the eldest, as my discretion almost warrants it, I say the mother shall out of the house or take such courses in it as shall sort with such a house and such a daughter.
Joan	Daughter, I say I will take any course so thou wilt leave thy passion; indeed it hurts thee, child. I'll sing and be merry, wear as fine clothes and as delicate dressings as thou wilt have me, so thou wilt pacify thyself and be at peace with me.
Winny	Oh, will you so? In so doing I may chance to look 160 upon you! Is this a fit habit for a handsome young gentlewoman's mother, as I hope to be a lady? You

look like one o' the Scottish weird sisters. Oh,
my heart has got the hiccup and all looks green
about me! A merry song now, mother, and thou
shalt be my white girl.

Joan   Ha, ha, ha! She's overcome with joy at my
conversion.

Doughty   [*aside*] She is most evidently bewitched.

Joan   (*sings*) There was a deft lad and a lass fell in love,   170
With a fa la la, fa la la, langtidown dilly.
With kissing and toying this maiden did prove,
With a fa la la, fa la la, langtidown dilly,
So wide i' th' waist and her belly so high,
That unto her mother the maiden did cry.
Oh langtidown dilly, Oh langtidown dilly,
Fa la la langtidown, langtidown dilly.

Enter PARNELL

Parnell   Thus would you do an I were dead. But while I
live you fadge not on it. Is this all the work you
can find?   180

Doughty   [*aside*] Now comes the maid to set her mistresses
to work!

Winny   Nay, prithee, sweet Parnell, I was but chiding the
old wife for her unhandsomeness, and would have
been at my work presently. She tells me now she
will wear fine things, and I shall dress her head as
I list.

Doughty   [*aside*] Here's a house well governed!

Parnell   Dress me no dressings, lessen I dress you both and

	learn a new lesson with a wanion right now. Ha' 190 I been a servant here this half dozen o' years, and can I see you idler than myself?
Joan & Winny	Nay, prithee, sweet Parnell, content and hark thee –
	[JOAN *and* WINNY *talk to Parnell aside*]
Doughty	[*aside*] I have known this, and till very lately, as well governed a family as the country yields, and now what a nest of several humours it is grown, and all devilish ones! Sure, all the witches in the country have their hands in this homespun medley, and there be no few, 'tis thought.
Parnell	Yea, yea, ye shall, ye shall, another time but not 200 now, I thank you. You shall as soon piss and paddle in't as slap me in the mouth with an old petticoat or a new pair o' shoen to be quiet. I cannot be quiet, nor I will not be quiet to see sicky doings, I.
Lawrence	Hold thy prattle, Parnell; all's come about as ween 'a' had it. Wot'st thou what, Parnell? Wot'st thou what? Oh dear, wot'st thou what?
Parnell	What's the fond waxen wild, trow I.
Lawrence	We ha' been in love these three years, and ever 210 we had not enough. Now is it come about that our love shall be at an end for ever and a day, for we mu' wed, my honey, we mu' wed.
Parnell	What the devil ails thee, limmer loon? Been thy brains broke loose, trow I.
Lawrence	Such a wedding was there never i' Lancashire as we'll couple at on Monday next.

Parnell	Aw, aw, say you this sickerly or done you but jam me?
Lawrence	I jam thee not nor flam thee not; 'tis all as true as 220 book. [*Shows a paper*] Here's both our masters have consented and concluded, and our mistresses mu' yield to't, to put all house and land and all they have into our hands.
Parnell	Aw, aw!
Lawrence	And we mu' marry and be master and dame of all!
Parnell	Aw, aw!
Lawrence	And they be our sojourners, because they are weary of the world, to live in friendliness and see 230 what will come on't
Parnell	Aw, aw, go on!
Seely & Gregory	Nay, 'tis true, Parnell; here's both our hands on't, and give you joy!
Joan & Winny	And ours too, and 'twill be fine i'fackins.
Parnell	Aw, aw, aw, aw!
Doughty	[*aside*] Here's a mad business towards!
Seely	I will bespeak the guests.
Gregory	And I the meat.
Joan	I'll dress the dinner, though I drip my sweat.
Lawrence	My care shall sumptuous 'pparelments provide. 240
Winny	And my best art shall trickly trim the bride.
Parnell	Aw, aw, aw, aw!

Gregory	I'll get choice music for the merriment.
Doughty	[*aside*] And I will wait with wonder the event!
Parnell	Aw, aw, aw, aw! *Exeunt*

ACT 2, SCENE 1

Enter four witches severally

All	Ho! Well met, well met.
Meg	What new device, what dainty strain,
	More for our mirth now than our gain,
	Shall we in practice put?
Moll	Nay, dame,
	Before we play another game
	We must a little laugh and thank
	Our feat familiars for the prank
	They played us last.
Mawd	Or they will miss
	Us in our next plot, if for this
	They find not their reward.
Meg	'Tis right.
Gillian	Therefore sing, Mawd, and call each sprite.

Enter four spirits

Mawd	[*Sings*] Come away, and take thy duggy.
Meg	Come, my Mamilion, like a puggy.
Mawd	And come, my Puckling, take thy teat,
	Your travails have deserv'd your meat.
Meg	Now, upon the churl's ground
	On which we're met, let's dance a round,
	That cockle, darnell, poppia wild

10

	May choke his grain and fill the field.	
Gillian	Now spirits fly about the task	20
	That we projected in our masque.	*Exit spirits*
Meg	Now let us laugh to think upon	
	The feat which we have so lately done,	
	In the distraction we have set	
	In Seely's house, which shall beget	
	Wonder and sorrow 'mongst our foes,	
	Whilst we make laughter of their woes.	
All	Ha, ha, ha!	
Meg	I can but laugh now to foresee	
	The fruits of their perplexity.	30
Gillian	Of Seely's family?	
Meg	Ay, ay, ay!	
	The father to the son doth cry,	
	The son rebukes the father old,	
	The daughter at the mother scold,	
	The wife the husband check and chide.	
	But that's no wonder, through the wide	
	World 'tis common!	
Gillian	But to be short,	
	The wedding must bring on the sport	
	Betwixt the hare-brain'd man and maid,	
	Master and dame that oversway'd.	40
All	Ha, ha, ha!	
Meg	Enough, enough!	
	Our sides are charm'd or else this stuff	
	Would laughter-crack them. Let's away	
	About the jig: we dance today	

	To spoil the hunters' sport.	
Gillian	Ay, that	
	Be now the subject of our chat.	
Meg	Then list ye well: the hunters are	
	This day by vow to kill a hare,	
	Or else the sport they will foreswear	50
	And hang their dogs up.	
Mawd	Stay, but where	
	Must the long-threaten'd hare be found?	
Gillian	They'll search in yonder meadow ground.	
Meg	There will I be, and like a wily wat,	
	Until they put me up, I'll squat.	
Gillian	I and my Puckling will a brace	
	Of greyhounds be, fit for the race,	
	And linger where we may be ta'en	
	Up for the course in the by-lane.	
	Then will we lead their dogs a-course,	60
	And every man and every horse,	
	Until they break their necks, and say –	
All	'The devil on Dun is rid this way!'	
	Ha, ha, ha, ha!	
Meg	All the doubt can be but this,	
	That if by chance of me they miss	
	And start another hare.	
Gillian	Then we'll not run,	
	But find some way how to be gone.	
	I shall know thee, Peg, by thy grizzled gut.	
Meg	And I you, Gillian, by your gaunt thin gut.	70
	But where will Mawd bestow herself today?	

Mawd	O' th' steeple-top I'll sit and see you play. *Exeunt*

[2.2]   Scene I

Enter GENEROUS, ARTHUR, BANTAM,
SHAKESTONE, *and* WHETSTONE

Generous   At meeting and at parting, gentlemen,
I only make use of that general word
So frequent at all feasts, and that but once:
You're 'welcome!'
You are so, all of you, and I entreat you
Take notice of that special business
Betwixt this gentleman (my friend) and I
About the mortgage, to which writings drawn
Your hands are witness.

Bantam & Shakestone   We acknowledge it.

Whetstone   My hand is there too, for a man cannot set to his   10
mark but it may be call'd his hand. I am a
gentleman both ways, and it hath been held that it
is the part of a gentleman to write a scurvy hand.

Bantam   You write, sir, like yourself.

Generous   Pray take no notice of his ignorance;
You know what I foretold you.

Arthur   'Tis confess'd.
But for that word by you so seldom spoke,
By us so freely on your part perform'd,
We hold us much engag'd.

Generous   I pray, no compliment;
It is a thing I do not use myself   20
Nor do I love't in others.

Arthur	For my part, Could I at once dissolve myself to words And after turn them into matter, such And of that strength as to attract the attention Of all the curious and most itching ears Of this our critic age, it could not make A theme amounting to your noble worth. You seem to me to supererogate, Supplying the defects of all your kindred, To ennoble your own name. I now have done, sir. 30
Whetstone	Hey day! This gentleman speaks like a country parson that had took his text out of Ovid's *Metamorphoses*.
Generous	[*To* ARTHUR] Sir, you hyperbolize. And I could chide you for't, but whilst you connive At this my kinsman I shall wink at you; 'Twill prove an equal match.
Arthur	Your name proclaims To be such as it speaks you: generous.
Generous	Still in that strain!
Arthur	Sir, sir, whilst you persevere to be good 40 I must continue grateful.
Generous	Gentlemen, The greatest part of this day you see is spent In reading deeds, conveyances, and bonds, With sealing and subscribing – will you now Take part of a bad supper?
Arthur	We are like travellers, And where such bait they do not use to inn. Our love and service to you.

Generous	The first I accept;
	The last I entertain not. Farewell, gentlemen.
Arthur	We'll try if we can find in our way home, 50
	When hares come from their coverts to relieve,
	A course or two.
Whetstone	Say you so, gentlemen? Nay then I am for your
	company still. 'Tis said hares are like
	hermaphrodites – one while male and another
	female – and that which begets this year brings
	young ones the next, which some think to be the
	reason that witches take their shapes so oft. Nay, if
	I lie, Pliny lies too – but come, now I have light
	upon you, I cannot so lightly leave you. Farewell, 60
	uncle.
Generous	Cousin, I wish you would consort yourself
	With such men ever and make them your precedent
	For a more gentle carriage.
Arthur	Good Master Generous – *Exeunt all but Generous*

Enter ROBERT

Generous	Robin!
Robert	Sir?
Generous	Go call your mistress hither.
Robert	My mistress, sir? I do call her 'mistress' as I do call
	you 'master', but if you would have me call my
	mistress to my master I may call loud enough
	before she can hear me. 70
Generous	Why, she's not deaf, I hope. I am sure since dinner

she had her hearing perfect.

Robert And so she may have at supper too for ought I
know, but I can assure you she is not now within
my call.

Generous Sirrah, you trifle. Give me the key o' th' stable,
I will go see my gelding. I' th' meantime
Go seek her out, say she shall find me there.

Robert To tell you true, sir, I shall neither find
My mistress here, nor you your gelding there.   80

Generous Ha? How comes that to pass?

Robert Whilst you were busy about your writings, she
came and commanded me to saddle your beast
and said she would ride abroad to take the air.

Generous Which of your fellows did she take along to wait
on her?

Robert None, sir.

Generous None? Hath she us'd it often?

Robert Oftener I am sure than she goes to church, and
leave out Wednesdays and Fridays.   90

Generous And still alone?

Robert If you call that alone, when nobody rides in her
company.

Generous But what times hath she sorted for these journeys?

Robert Commonly when you are abroad, and sometimes
when you are full of business at home.

Generous To ride out often and alone! What saith she
When she takes horse, and at her back return?

Robert	Only conjures me that I shall keep it from you,
	then claps me in the fist with some small piece of 100
	silver, and then a fish cannot be more silent that I.

Generous	I know her a good woman and well bred,
	Of an unquestion'd carriage, well reputed
	Amongst her neighbours, reckon'd with the best
	And o'er me most indulgent, though in many
	Such things might breed a doubt and jealousy,
	Yet I hatch no such frenzy. Yet to prevent
	The smallest jar that might betwixt us happen,
	Give her no notice that I know thus much.
	Besides, I charge thee, when she craves him next 110
	He be denied. If she be vex'd or mov'd,
	Do not thou feare: I'll interpose myself
	Betwixt thee and her anger. As you tender
	Your duty and my service, see this done.

Robert	Now you have expressed your mind I know what
	I have to do: first, not to tell her what I have told
	you, and next to keep her side-saddle from
	coming upon your gelding's back. But, howsoever,
	it is like to hinder me of many a round tester.

| Generous | As oft as thou deny'st her, so oft claim   120 |
| | That tester from me; 't shall be roundly paid. |

Robert	You say well in that, sir. I dare take your word –
	you are an honest gentleman and my master – and
	now take mine as I am your true servant: before
	she shall back your gelding again in your absence,
	while I have the charge of his keeping, she shall
	ride me or I'll ride her!

| Generous | So much for that. Sirrah, my butler tells me |
| | My cellar is drunk dry – I mean those bottles |

	Of sack and claret are all empty grown	130
	And I have guests tomorrow, my choice friends.	
	Take the grey nag i' th' stable and those bottles	
	Fill at Lancaster, there where you use to fetch it.	
Robert	[aside] Good news for me! – I shall sir.	
Generous	Oh Robin, it comes short of that pure liquor	
	We drunk last term in London at the Mitre	
	In Fleet Street – thou rememberest it? Methought	
	It was the very spirit of the grape,	
	Mere quintessence of wine!	
Robert	Yes, sir, I so remember it that most certain it is I	140
	never shall forget it; my mouth waters ever since	
	when I but think on't. Whilst you were at supper	
	above, the drawer had me down into the cellar	
	below – I know the way in again if I see't – but at	
	that time to find the way out again I had the help	
	of more eyes than mine own. Is the taste of that	
	Ipsitate still in your palate, sir?	
Generous	What then? But vain are wishes. Take those bottles	
	And see them fill'd where I command you, sir.	
Robert	I shall. [aside] Never could I have met with such a	150
	fair opportunity, for just in the mid way lies my	
	sweetheart, as lovely a lass as any is in Lancashire,	
	and kisses as sweetly. I'll see her going or coming;	
	I'll have one smooch at thy lips and be with thee	
	to bring, Moll Spencer.	*Exit*
Generous	Go, hasten your return. What he hath told me	
	Touching my wife is somewhat strange. No matter.	
	Be't as it will, it shall not trouble me.	
	She hath not lain so long so near my side	

That now I should be jealous.]   160

Enter a SOLDIER

Soldier	You seem, sir, a gentlemen of quality and no doubt but in your youth have been acquainted with affairs military. In your very looks there appears bounty and in your person humanity. Please you to vouchsafe the tender of some small courtesy to help to bear a soldier into his country.

Generous   Though I could tax you friend, and justly too,
              For begging 'gainst the statute in that name,
              Yet I have ever been of that compassion,
              Where I see want, rather to pity it   170
              Than to use power. Where hast thou served?

Soldier   With the Russian against the Polack, a heavy war
              and hath brought me to this hard fate. I was took
              prisoner by the Pole and, after some few weeks of
              durance, got both my freedom and pass. I have it
              about me to show; please you to vouchsafe the
              perusal?

Generous   It shall not need. What countryman?

Soldier   Yorkshire, sir. Many a sharp battle by land, and
              many a sharp storm at sea, many a long mile, and   180
              many a short meal, I have travelled and suffered
              ere I could reach thus far. I beseech you, sir, take
              my poor and wretched case into your worship's
              noble consideration.

Generous   Perhaps thou lov'st this wandering life,
              To be an idle loitering beggar, than

	To eat of thine own labour.
Soldier	I, sir? Loitering I defy, sir! I hate laziness as I do leprosy; it is the next way to breed the scurvy. Put me to hedge, ditch, plough, thresh, dig, delve, 190 anything: your worship shall find that I love nothing less than loitering.
Generous	Friend, thou speakest well.

Enter MILLER, *his hands and face scratched and bloody*

Miller	'Your mill', quoth he! If ever you take me in your mill again, I'll give you leave to cast my flesh to the dogs and grind my bones to powder betwixt the millstones. 'Cats' do you call them? For their hugeness they might be cat o' mountains, and for their claws I think I have it here in red and white to show. I pray look here, sir. A murrain take 200 them. I'll be sworn they have scratched where I am sure it itched not.
Generous	How camest thou in this pickle?
Miller	You see, sir, and what you see I have felt, and am come to give you to understand I'll not endure such another night if you would give me your mill for nothing. They say we millers are thieves, but I could as soon be hanged as steal one piece of a nap all the night long. Good landlord, provide yourself of a new tenant. The noise of such caterwauling, 210 and such scratching and clawing, before I would endure again, I'll be tied to the sail when the wind blows sharpest and they fly swiftest till I be torn torn into as many fitters as I have toes and fingers.

Soldier	I was a miller myself before I was a soldier. What one of my own trade should be so poorly spirited, frighted with cats?
	Sir, trust me with the mill that he forsakes.
	Here is a blade that hangs upon this belt
	That spite of all these rats, cats, weasels, witches, 220
	Or dogs, or devils, shall so conjure them
	I'll quiet my possession.
Generous	Well spoke, soldier!
	I like thy resolution. [*To* MILLER] Fellow, you then
	Have given the mill quite over?
Miller	Over and over. Here I utterly renounce it, nor would I stay in it longer if you would give me your whole estate. Nay, if I say it you may take my word, landlord.
Soldier	I pray, sir, dare you trust your mill with me?
Generous	I dare, but I am loath, my reasons these: 230
	For many months scarce anyone hath lain there
	But have been strangely frighted in his sleep,
	Or from his warm bed drawn into the floor,
	Or claw'd and scratch'd as thou see'st this poor man,
	So much that it stood long untenanted,
	Till he late undertook it. Now thine eyes
	Witness how he hath sped.
Soldier	Give me the keys; I'll stand it all danger.
Generous	'Tis a match. [*To* MILLER] Deliver them.
Miller	Marry, with all my heart, and I am glad I am so rid 240 of 'em. *Exeunt*

Scene III

[2.3]

Enter BOY *with a switch*

Boy   Now I have gathered bullace and filled my belly
pretty well, I'll go see some sport. There are
gentlemen coursing in the meadow hard by,
and 'tis a game I love better than going to school,
ten to one.

*Enter an invisible spirit (John Adson) with a brace
of greyhounds*

What have we here – a brace of greyhounds broke
loose from their masters? It must needs be so, for
they have both their collars and slips about their
necks. Now I look better upon them, methinks I
should know them, and so I do: these are Master   10
Robinson's dogs, that dwells some two miles off.
I'll take them up and lead them home to their
master; it may be something in my way for he is
as liberal a gentlemen as any is in our country. [*To
one of the dogs*] Come, Hector, come. Now if I
could but start a hare by the way, kill her and carry
her home to my supper, I should think I had made
a better afternoon's work of it than gathering
bullace. Come, poor curs, along with me.   *Exeunt*

[2.4]   *Scene IV.*

Enter ARTHUR, BANTAM, SHAKESTONE,
and WHETSTONE

Arthur	My dog as yours.
Shakestone	For what?
Arthur	A piece.
Shakestone	'Tis done.
Bantam	I say the pied dog shall outstrip the brown.
Whetstone	And I'll take the brown dog's part against the pied.
Bantam	Yes, when he's at his lap you'll take his part.
Arthur	Bantam, forbear him prithee.
Bantam	He talks so like an ass; I have not patience to endure his nonsense!
Whetstone	The brown dog for two pieces.
Bantam	Of what?
Whetstone	Of what you dare! Name them from the last farthings, with the double rings, to the late-coined pieces which they say are all counterfeit.
Bantam	Well, sir, I take on. [*Shows him coins*] Will you cover these? Give them into the hands of either of those two gentlemen.
Whetstone	What needs that? Do you think my word and my money is not all one?
Bantam	And weigh alike – both many grains too light.
Shakestone	Enough of that. I presume, Master Whetstone, you are not ignorant what belongs to the sport of

10

20

	hunting?
Whetstone	I think I have reason, for I have been at the death of more hares –
Bantam	More than you shed the last fall of the leaf.
Whetstone	More than any man here I am sure. I should be loath at these years to be ignorant of haring or whoring. I knew a hare, close hunted, climb a tree.
Bantam	To find out birds' nests!
Whetstone	Another leap into a river, nothing appearing above water save only the tip of her nose to take breath. 30
Shakestone	Nay that's very likely, for no man can fish with an angle but his line must be made of hair.
Whetstone	You say right! I knew another who to escape the dogs hath taken a house and leapt in at a window.
Bantam	It is thought you came into the world that way.
Whetstone	How mean you that?
Bantam	Because you are a bastard.
Whetstone	Bastard? O, base!
Bantam	And thou art base all over.
Arthur	Needs must I now condemn your indiscretion, 40 To set your wit against his!
Whetstone	'Bastard'? That shall be tried. Well, gentlemen, concerning hare hunting, you might have heard more if he had had the grace to have said less. But for the word 'bastard', if I do not tell my uncle, ay, and my aunt too, either when I would speak ought or go off the score for anything, let me never be

trusted. They are older than I, and what know I but they might be by when I was begot. But if thou, Bantam, dost not hear of this with both thine ears, if thou hast them still, and not lost them by scribbling, instead of Whetstone call me Grindstone, and for By-blow, Bullfinch. Gentlemen, for two of you, your company is fair and honest, but for you, Bantam, remember and take notice also that I am a bastard, and so much I'll testify to my aunt and uncle.   *Exit*   50

Arthur   What have you done? 'Twill grieve the good old gentleman to hear him baffled thus.

Bantam   I was in a cold sweat ready to faint   60
              The time he stayed amongst us.

Shakestone But come; now the hare is found and started! She shall have law. So to our sport!   *Exeunt*

[2.5]   Scene V.

                    Enter BOY *with the greyhounds*

Boy   A hare, a hare! Halloo, halloo! The devil take these curs; will they not stir? Halloo, halloo! There, there, there! What, are they grown so lither and so lazy? Are Master Robinson's dogs turned tykes with a wanion? The hare is yet in sight, halloo, halloo! Marry, hang you for a couple of mongrels (if you were worth hanging), and have you served me thus? Nay, then, I'll serve you with the like sauce: you shall to the next bush, there will I tie you, and use you like a couple of curs as you are,   10
              and, though not lash you, yet lash you whilst my switch will hold. Nay, since you have left your

speed, I'll see if I can put spirit into you and put
you in remembrance what 'halloo, halloo!'
means.

As he beats them, there appears before him [GILLIAN]
Dickinson and [*a small demon-child in place of the
greyhounds*]

Now, bless me heaven! One of the greyhounds
turned into a woman, the other into a boy! The
lad I never saw before, but her I know well: it is
my gammer Dickinson.

Gillian	Sirrah, you have serv'd me well to swinge me thus!	20
	You young rogue, you have us'd me like a dog!	

Boy   When you had put yourself into a dog's skin, I
pray how could I help it? But gammer, are not you
a witch? [*He kneels*] If you be, I beg upon my
knees you will not hurt me.

Gillian   Stand up, my boy, for thou shalt have no harm.
Be silent, speak of nothing thou hast seen,
And here's a shilling for thee.

Boy   I'll have none of your money, gammer, because
you are a witch! [*aside*] And now she is out of her   30
four-legged shape, I'll see if with my two legs I can
outrun her! [*He runs away*]

Gillian   Nay, sirrah, though you be young, and I old,
You are not so nimble, nor I so lame,
But I can overtake you. [*She seizes him*]

Boy   But gammer, what do you mean to do with me
now you have me?

Gillian	To hug thee, stroke thee, and embrace thee thus,
	And teach thee twenty thousand pretty things,
	So thou tell no tales. And, boy, this night 40
	Thou must along with me to a brave feast.

Boy   Not I, gammer, indeed, la. I dare not stay out late.
My father is a fell man, and, if I be out long, will
both chide and beat me.

Gillian   'Not', sirrah? Then perforce thou shalt along.
This bridle helps me still at need,
And shall provide us of a steed.
[*To the demon-child*] Now, sirrah, take your shape and be
Prepar'd to hurry him and me. –
Now look and tell me what's the lad become?   50

> [*The demon-child*] exit[*s and* BOY *peers through the
> stage door after him*]

Boy   The boy is vanished, and I can see nothing in his
stead but a white horse, ready saddled and bridled.

Gillian   And that's the horse we must bestride,
On which both thou and I must ride,
Thou, boy, before and I behind,
The earth we tread not, but the wind.
For we must progress through the air,
And I will bring thee to such fare
As thou ne'er sawst, up and away,
For now no longer we can stay.   60

Boy   Help! Help!

> *She catches him up, and turning round,* [*they*] *exit*

[2.6]

Scene 6

Enter ROBERT *and* MOLL

Robert   Thanks, my sweet Moll, for thy courteous
entertainment: thy cream, thy cheese-cakes, and
every good thing. ([*He*] *kiss*[*es her*]) This, this, and
this for all!

Moll   But why in such haste, good Robin?

Robert   I confess my stay with thee is sweet to me, but I
must spur Cut the faster for't to be at home in the
morning. I have yet to Lancaster to ride tonight,
and this my bandolier of bottles to fill tonight, and
then half a score mile to ride by curry-comb time   10
in the morning, or the old man chides, Moll.

Moll   He shall not chide thee; fear it not.

Robert   Pray Bacchus I may please him with his wine,
which will be the hardest thing to do, for, since he
was last at London and tasted the divinity of the
Mitre, scarce any liquor in Lancashire will go
down with him. Sure, sure, he will never be a
puritan, he holds so well with the Mitre.

Moll   Well, Robert, I find your love by your haste from
me. I'll undertake you shall be at Lancaster, and   20
twice as far, and yet at home time enough, an be
ruled by me.

Robert   Thou art a witty rogue, and think'st to make me
believe anything because I saw thee make thy
broom sweep the house without hands t'other
day!

Moll   You shall see more than that presently, because

| | you shall believe me. You know the house is all a-bed here, and I dare not be missed in the morning. Besides, I must be at the wedding of Lawrence and Parnell tomorrow. | 30 |

| Robert | Ay, your old sweetheart Lawrence! Old love will not be forgotten. |

| Moll | I care not for the loss of him, but if I fit him not, hang me. But to the point: if I go with you tonight and help you to as good wine as your master desires, and you keep your time with him, you will give me a pint for my company? |

| Robert | Thy belly-ful, wench! |

| Moll | I'll but take up my milk-pail and leave it in the field till our coming back in the morning, and we'll away. | 40 |

| Robert | Go fetch it quickly, then. |

| Moll | No, Robert, rather than leave your company so long, it shall come to me. |

| Robert | I would but see that! (*The pail goes* [*towards* MOLL]) |

| Moll | Look yonder, what do you think on't? |

| Robert | Light, it comes! And I do think there is so much of the devil in't as will turn all the milk shall come in't these seven years, and make it burn too till it stink worse than the proverb of the bishop's foot! | 50 |

| Moll | Look you, sir! [*She grasps the pail*] Here, I have it. Will you get up and away? |

| Robert | [*Looking through doorway*] My horse is gone! Nay, prithee, Moll, thou has set him away; leave thy |

	roguery!
Moll	Look again.
Robert	There stands a black long-sided jade; mine was a trussed grey!
Moll	Yours was too short to carry double such a 60 journey. Get up, I say, you shall have your own again i' th' morning.
Robert	Nay but, nay but –
Moll	Nay, an you stand butting now, I'll leave you to look your horse. Pail, on afore to the field and stay till I come. [*She puts down the pail and it goes out the door*]
Robert	Come away, then. Hey for Lancaster. Stand up! *Exeunt*

ACT 3, SCENE 1

Enter SEELY *and* JOAN, *his wife*

Seely   Come away, wife, come away, and let us be ready
             to break the cake over the bride's head at her
             entrance. We will have the honour of it, we that
             have played the steward and cook at home, though
             we lost church by't and saw not Parson Knit-Knot
             do his office. But we shall see all the house-rites
             performed and – oh what a day of jollity and
             tranquility is here towards!

Joan   You are so frolic and so crank now, upon the truce
             is taken amongst us because our wrangling shall   10
             not wrong the wedding. But take heed, you were
             best, how ye behave yourself, lest a day to come
             may pay for all!

Seely   I fear nothing, and I hope to die in this humour.

Joan   Oh, how hot am I! I'd rather than I would dress
             such another dinner this twelve month, I would
             wish 'wedding' quite out of this year's almanac.

Seely   I'll fetch a cup of sack, wife.   [*Exit*]

Joan   How brag he is of his liberty, but the holiday
             carries it.   20

[Enter SEELY *with a cup]*

Seely   [*Hands her the cup*] Here, here, sweetheart. They
             are long, methinks, a-coming. The bells have rung

out this half hour; hark now the wind brings the
sound of them sweetly again!

Joan   They ring backwards, methinks.

Seely   I'fack they do! Sure the greatest fire in the parish is
in our kitchen and there's no harm done yet – no
'tis some merry conceit of the stretch-ropes, the
ringers. Now they have done, and now the
wedding comes – hark, the fiddlers and all! Now   30
have I lived to see a day! Come, take our stand and
be ready for the bride-cake, which we will so crack
and crumble upon her crown. Oh, they come,
they come!

Enter [fiddlers, leading the married couple]
LAWRENCE [*and*] PARNELL, [*attended by*]
WINNY, MOLL, [*and*] *two country lasses,* [*then*]
DOUGHTY, GREGORY, ARTHUR,
SHAKESTONE, BANTAM, *and* WHETSTONE

All   Joy, health, and children to the married pair!

Lawrence & Parnell   We thank you all.

Lawrence   So pray come in and fare.

Parnell   As well as we, and taste of every cate.

Lawrence   With bonny bridegroom and his lovely mate!

Arthur   This begins bravely.

Doughty   They agree better than the bells e'en now. 'Slid   40
they rung tunably well till we were all out of the
church, and then they clattered as the devil had
been in the belfry. On, in the name of wedlock,

fiddlers, on!

Lawrence   On with your melody!
            The fiddlers pass through, and play the battle [as they exit]

Bantam   Enter the gates with joy,
            And as you enter play 'The Sack of Troy'.

            [Enter a] spirit [above]

Joan   Welcome, bride Parnell.

Seely   Bridegroom Lawrence eke.
            [To LAWRENCE]
            In you before, for we this cake must break
            Over the bride –   *[Exit* LAWRENCE]

            As they lift up the cake, the spirit snatches it and
            pours down bran

            Forgi' me! What's become o' th' cake, wife?   50

Joan   It slipped out of my hand and is fallen into
            crumbs, I think.

Doughty   [*aside*] 'Crumbs?' The devil of crumb is here – but
            bran, nothing but bran? What prodigy is this?

Parnell   Is my best bride's cake come to this? Oh, woe
            worth it!

            Exit PARNELL, SEELY, JOAN, *and maids*

Whetstone   How daintily the bride's hair is powder'd with it!

Arthur   My hair stands on end to see it!

Bantam   And mine!

Shakestone	I was never so amaz'd!
Doughty	What can it mean?
Gregory	Pax, I think not on't! 'Tis but some of my father 60 and mother's roguery. This is a law-day with 'em, to do what they list.
Whetstone	I never fear anything so long as my aunt has but bidden me think of her, and she'll warrant me.
Doughty	Well, gentlemen, let's follow the rest in and fear Nothing yet. The house smells well of good cheer!

Enter SEELY

Seely	Gentlemen, will it please you draw near? The guests are now all come and the house almost full, meat's taken up –
Doughty	We were now coming. 70
Seely	But son Gregory, nephew Arthur, and the rest of the young gentlemen, I shall take it for a favour if you will – it is an office which very good gentlemen do in this country – accompany the bridegroom in serving the meat.
All	With all our hearts!
Seely	Nay, neighbour Doughty, your years shall excuse you.
Doughty	Pah! I am not so old but I can carry more meat than I can eat. If the young rascals could carry 80 their drink as well, the country would be quieter.

Knocking within, as [upon a] dresser

Seely	Well, fare your hearts. The dresser calls in,
	gentlemen. *Exeunt [all but* SEELY]
	'Tis a busy time, yet will I review the bill of fare
	for this day's dinner.
	[*Taking a paper from his pocket, he*] *reads*
	'For forty people of the best quality, four messes
	of meat, *viz*: a leg of mutton in plum broth, a dish
	of marrowbones, a capon in white broth, a sirloin
	of beef, a pig, a goose, a turkey, and two pies. For
	the second course: to every mess four chickens in 90
	a dish, a couple of rabbits, custard, flan,
	Florentines, and stewed prunes.'
	All very good country fare, and for my credit –

          Enter [fiddlers] playing [followed by] LAWRENCE,
          DOUGHTY, ARTHUR, SHAKESTONE,
          BANTAM, WHETSTONE, AND GREGORY,
          [*all carrying covered*] *dishes.* [*The*] *spirit* [*above casts a*
          spell on] *the dishes as they enter.*

	The service enters – Oh, well said music!
	Play up the meat to' th' table till all be serv'd in;
	I'll see it pass in answer to my bill.
Doughty	Hold up you head, Master Bridegroom!
Lawrence	On afore, fiddlers, my doubler cools in my hands.
Seely	[*Reading his bill*] '*Imprimis*: A leg of mutton in
	plum broth' – How now, Master Bridegroom, 100
	what carry you?
Lawrence	'Twere hot e'en now, but now it's cold as a stone!

[SEELY *uncovers* LAWRENCE's *dish to reveal a ram's horn*]

Seely	A stone? 'Tis horn, man!
Lawrence	Aw! *Exit Fiddlers*
Seely	It was mutton, but now 'tis the horns on't.
Lawrence	Aw, where's my bride? *Exit*

[DOUGHTY, ARTHUR, SHAKESTONE, BANTAM, AND WHETSTONE *uncover their dishes*]

Doughty	'Zooks, I brought as good a sirloin of beef from the dresser as knife could be put to, and see! – I'll stay i' this house no longer!
Arthur	And if this were not a capon in white broth, I am 110 one i' the coop!
Shakestone	All, all's transform'd! Look you what I have!
Bantam	And I!
Whetstone	And I! Yet I fear nothing, thank my aunt.
Gregory	I had a pie that is not open'd yet. I'll see what's in that –

[*He lifts the pie-crust and birds fly out*]

Live birds, as true as I live – look where they fly! *Exit spirit*

Doughty	Witches, live witches! The house is full of witches! If we love our lives, let's out on't.

Enter JOAN *and* WINNY

Joan	O husband! O guests! O son! O gentlemen! 120

Joan
O husband! O guests! O son! O gentlemen!   120
Such a chance in a kitchen was never heard of. All
the meat is flown out o' the chimney top, I think,
and nothing instead of it but snakes, bats, frogs,
beetles, hornets, and humble-bees. All the salads
are turned to Jew's-ears, mushrooms, and
puckfists, and all the custards into cow-shards!

Doughty
What shall we do? Dare we stay any longer?

Arthur
'Dare we'? Why not? I defy all witches,
And all their works; their power on our meat
Cannot reach our persons.

Whetstone
                                    I say so too,   130
And so my aunt ever told me, so long
I will fear nothing. Be not afraid, Master Doughty.

Doughty
'Zooks! I fear nothing living that I can
See more than you, and that's nothing at all.
But to think of these invisible mischiefs
Troubles me, I confess.

Arthur
Sir, I will not go about to over-rule your reason,
but for my part I will not out of a house on a
bridal day, till I see the last man borne.

Doughty
'Zooks! Thou art so brave a fellow that I will stick   140
to thee, and if we come off handsomely – I am an
old bachelor, thou knowst, and must have an
heir – I like thy spirit! Where's the bride? Where's
the bridegroom? Where's the music? Where be the
lasses? Ha' you any wine i' the house? Though we
make no dinner, let's try if we can make an
afternoon.

Joan	Nay, sir, if you please to stay – now that the many are frighted away – I have some good cold meats and half a dozen bottles of wine. 150
Seely	And I will bid you welcome.
Doughty	Say you me so, but will not your son be angry and your daughter chide you?
Gregory	Fear not you that, sir, for look you I obey my father.
Winny	And I my mother.
Joan	And we are all at this instant as well and as sensible of our former errors as you can wish us to be.
Doughty	Nay, if the witches have but robbed of your meat, 160 and restored your reason, here has been no hurt done today. But this is strange, and as great a wonder as the rest to me.
Arthur	It seems though these hags had power to make the wedding cheer a *deceptio visus*, the former store has 'scaped 'em.
Doughty	I am glad on't, but the devil good 'em with my sirloin. [*aside*] I thought to have set that by mine own trencher – But you have cold meat, you say?
Joan	Yes, sir! 170
Doughty	And wine, you say?
Joan	Yes, sir!
Doughtly	I hope the country wenches and the fiddlers are not gone?
Winny	They are all here, and one the merriest wench that

	makes all the rest so laugh and tickle.
Seely	Gentlemen, will you in?
All	Agreed on all parts!
Doughty	If not a wedding, we will make a wake on't, and away with the witch. I fear nothing now you have 180 your wits again. But look you hold 'em while you have 'em! *Exeunt*

[3.2]

Enter GENEROUS, *and* ROBERT *with a paper*

Generous	I confess thou hast done a wonder in fetching me so good wine, but, my good servant Robert, go not about to put a miracle upon me. I will rather believe that Lancaster affords this wine – which I thought impossible till I tasted it – than that thou couldst in one night fetch it from London.
Robert	I have known when you have held me for an honest fellow, and would have believed me.
Generous	Th'art a knave to wish me to believe this. Forgi' me. I would have sworn, if thou hadst stayed but 10 time answerable for the journey (to his that flew to Paris and back to London in a day), it had been the same wine. But it can never fall within the compass of a Christian's belief that thou couldst ride above three hundred miles in eight hours: you were no longer out, and upon one horse too, and in the night too!
Robert	[*aside*] And carry a wench behind me too, and did something else too, but I must not speak of her

	lest I be devil-torn.	20

Generous And fill thy bottles too, and come home half drunk too, for so thou art, thou wouldst never 'a' had such a fancy else!

Robert I am sorry I have said so much, and not let Lancaster have the credit o' the wine.

Generous Oh, are you so? And why have you abused me and yourself, then, all this while to glorify The Mitre in Fleet Street?

Robert I could say, sir, that you might have the better opinion of the wine, for there are a great many palates in the kingdom that can relish no wine unless it be of such a tavern, and drawn by such a drawer – 30

Generous I said, and I say again: if I were within ten mile of London, I durst swear that this was Mitre wine, and drawn by honest Jack Paine.

Robert Nay then, sir, I swore, and I swear again: honest Jack Paine drew it.

Generous Ha, ha, ha! If I could believe there were such a thing as witchcraft, I should think this slave were bewitched now with an opinion. 40

Robert Much good do you, sir, your wine and your mirth, and my place for your next groom; I desire not to stay to be laughed out of my opinion.

Generous Nay, be not angry Robin, we must not part so. And how does my honest drawer? Ha, ha, ha! And what news at London, Robin? Ha, ha, ha! But your stay was so short I think you could hear

| | none, and such your haste home that you could make none; is't not so, Robin? Ha, ha, ha! [*aside*] What a strange fancy has good wine begot in his head? *Drunken.* | 50 |

Robert [*aside*] Now will I push him over and over with a piece of paper. – Yes, sir, I have brought you something from London.

Generous Come on, now, let me hear.

Robert Your honest drawer, sir, considering that you considered him well for his good wine –

Generous [*aside*] What shall we hear now?

Robert Was very careful to keep or convey this paper to you, which it seems you dropped in the room there.

Generous [*aside*] Bless me! This paper belongs to me indeed, 'tis an acquittance, and all I have to show for the payment of one hundred pound. I took great care for 't, and could not imagine where or how I might lose it. But why may not this be a trick? This knave may find it when I lost it, and conceal it till now to come over me withal. I will not trouble my thoughts with it further at this time. – Well, Robin, look to your business, and have a care of my gelding.   *Exit*

Robert Yes, sir. I think I have nettled him now, but not as I was nettled last night: three hundred miles a night upon a raw-boned devil (as, in my heart, it was a devil), and then a wench that shared more o' my back than the said devil did o' my bum. This is rank riding, my masters. But why had I such an

itch to tell my master of it, and that he should
believe it? I do now wish that I had not told, and   80
that he will not believe it, for I dare not tell him
the means. 'Sfoot, my wench and her friends the
fiends will tear me to pieces if I discover her. A
notable rogue, she's at the wedding now, for as
good a maid as the best o 'em –

Enter MISTRESS GENEROUS *with a bridle*

Oh, my mistress!

Mrs Generous	Robin?
Robert	Ay, mistress?
Mrs Generous	Quickly, good Robin, the grey gelding.
Robert	What other horse you please, mistress. 90
Mrs Generous	And why not that?
Robert	Truly, mistress, pray pardon me, I must be plain with you: I dare not deliver him you. My master has ta'en notice of the ill case you have brought him home in diverse times.
Mrs Generous	Oh, is it so? And must he be made acquainted with my actions by you, and must I then be controlled by him, and now by you? You are a saucy groom!
Robert	You may say your pleasure. *(He turns from her)* 100
Mrs Generous	No, sir, I'll do my pleasure. *(She bridles him)*
Robert	Aw!
Mrs Generous	'Horse, horse, see thou be,

And where I point thee carry me.'

Exeunt, [he] neighing

Scene 3

[3.3]

Enter ARTHUR, SHAKESTONE, AND BANTAM

Arthur   Was there ever such a medley of mirth, madness, and drunkenness shuffled together?

Shakestone   Thy uncle and aunt, old Master Seely and his wife, do nothing but kiss and play together like monkeys.

Arthur   Yes, they do over-love one another now.

Bantam   And young Gregory and his sister do as much overdo their obedience now to their parents.

Arthur   And their parents as much over-dote upon them. They are all as far beyond their wits now in loving   10 one another as they were wide of them before in crossing.

Shakestone   Yet this is the better madness.

Bantam   But the married couple that are both so daintily whittled, that now they are both mad to be a-bed before supper-time – And by and by he will, and she won't, straight she will and he won't; the next minute they both forget they are married and defy one another.

Arthur   My sides e'en ache with laughter!   20

Shakestone   But the best sport of all is, the old bachelor Master Doughty, that was so cautious and feared every

	thing to be witchcraft, is now wound up to such a confidence that there is no such thing that he dares the devil do his worst, and will not out o' the house by all persuasion, and all for the love of the husbandman's daughter within, Moll Spencer.
Arthur	[aside] There I am in some danger. He put me into half a belief I shall be his heir; pray love she be not a witch to charm his love from me. – Of what condition is that wench? Dost thou know her?

30

Shakestone	A little, but Whetstone knows her better.
Arthur	Hang him rogue! He'll belie her and speak better than she deserves, for he's in love with her too. I saw old Doughty give him a box o' the ear for kissing her, and he turned about, as he did by thee yesterday, and swore his aunt should know it.
Bantam	Who would ha' thought that impudent rogue would have come among us after such a baffle?
Shakestone	He told me he had complained to his aunt on us, and that she would speak with us.

40

Arthur	We will all to her to patch up the business, for the respect I bear her husband, noble Generous.
Bantam	Here he comes.

Enter WHETSTONE

Arthur	Hark you, Master By-blow, do you know the lass within? What do you call her, Moll Spencer?
Whetstone	Sir, what I know I'll keep to myself. A good, civil, merry, harmless rogue she is, and comes to my

aunt often, and that's all I know by her.

Arthur   You do well to keep it to yourself, sir!   50

Whetstone   And you may do well to question her, if you dare,
                for the testy old coxcomb that will not let her go
                out of his hand.

Shakestone   Take heed, he's at your heels.

                Enter DOUGHTY, MOLL, and two country lasses

Doughty   Come away, wenches – where are you, gentlemen?
                Play, fiddlers, [*To* MOLL] let's have a dance, ha,
                my little rogue! (*Kisses* MOLL) 'Zooks, what ails
                thy nose?

Moll   My nose? Nothing sir. (*Turns about*) Yet me
                thought a fly touched it. Did you see anything?   60

Doughty   No, no, yet I would almost ha' sworn – I would
                not have sprite or goblin blast thy face, for all their
                kingdom. But hang't there is no such thing.
                Fiddlers, will you play?

                [*Fiddlers above begin*] 'Sellenger's Round'

                Gentlemen, will you dance?

All   With all our hearts.

Arthur   But stay, where's this household,
                This family of love? Let's have them into the
                revels.

Doughty   [*To the fiddlers*] Hold a little, then.

Shakestone   Here they come all
                In a true-love knot.   70

Enter SEELY, JOAN, GREGORY, [*and*] WINNY

Gregory	O father, twenty times a day is too little to ask you blessing.
Seely	Go to, you are a rascal! (*To* JOAN) And you, housewife, teach your daughter better manners. – I'll ship you all for New England else.
Bantam	The knot's untied, and this is another change.
Joan	Yes, I will teach her manners, or put her out to spin two-penny tow, so you, dear husband, will but take me into favour. (*To* WINNY) I'll talk with you, dame, when the strangers are gone. 80
Gregory	Dear father.
Winny	Dear mother.
Gregory & Winny	Dear father and mother, pardon us but This time.
Seely & Joan	Never, and therefore hold your peace!
Doughty	Nay, that's unreasonable.
Gregory & Winny	Oh! ([*They*] *weep*)
Seely	But for your sake I'll forbear them, and bear with anything this day.
Arthur	[*To* DOUGHTY] Do you note this? Now they are all worse than ever they were, in a contrary vein. What think you of witchcraft now? 90
Doughty	They are all natural fools, man, I find it now. Art thou mad, to dream of witchcraft?
Arthur	[*aside*] He's as much changed and bewitched as

	they, I fear.
Doughty	Hey day! Here comes the pair of boiled lovers in sorrel sops.

Enter LAWRENCE *and* PARNELL

Lawrence	Nay, dear honey, nay honey, but once, once.
Parnell	No, no, I ha' sworn, I ha' sworn: not a bit afore bed. And look you, it's but now dancing time.
Doughty	Come away, bridegroom, we'll stay your stomach 100 with a dance. [*To the fiddlers above*] Now, masters, play a-good. [*To* MOLL] Come, my lass, we'll shown them how 'tis.

[Fiddlers above begin] 'Sellenger's Round' [again]. As [the guests] begin to dance, they play another tune, then [each plays a different tune]

Arthur, Bantam, & Shakestone	Whither now, ho!
Doughty	Hey day! Why, you rogues.
Whetstone	What, does the devil ride o' your fiddlesticks?
Doughty	You drunken rogues, hold, hold I say, and begin again soberly 'The Beginning of the World'.

[The fiddlers start again, each playing a different tune]

Arthur, Bantam, & Shakestone	Ha, ha, ha, how's this?
Bantam	Every one a several tune! 110
Doughty	This is something towards it. I bade them play 'The Beginning of the World', and they play I

	know not what.	
Arthur	No, 'tis 'The Running o' the Country' several ways. But what do you think on't? (*Music cease[s]*)	
Doughty	'Think'? I think they are drunk. Prithee do not thou think of witchcraft. For my part, I shall as soon think this maid one, as that there's any in Lancashire.	
Moll	Ha, ha, ha!	120
Doughty	Why dost thou laugh?	
Moll	To think this bridegroom should once ha' been mine, but he shall rue it. [*She produces a point*] I'll hold him this point on't, and that's all I care for him.	
Doughty	A witty rogue.	
Whetstone	I tell you sir, they say she made a pail follow her t'other day up two pair of stairs.	
Doughty	You lying rascal!	
Arthur	O sir, forget your anger.	130
Moll	Look you, Master Bridegroom, what my care provides for you.	
Lawrence	What, a point?	
Moll	Yes, put it in your pocket. It may stand you in stead anon, when all your points are ta'en away, to truss up your trinkets, I mean your slops, withal.	
Lawrence	Moll, for old acquaintance I will ma' thy point a point of preferment. [*He attaches it to his cod-piece*] It sha' be the foreman of a whole jury o' points,	

	and right here will I wear it.	140
Parnell	Wi' ya? Wi' ya? Old love wi' no be forgotten, but I's never be jealous the more for that!	
Arthur	Play, fiddlers, anything!	
Doughty	Ay, and let's see your faces, that you play fairly with us.	

Musicians show themselves above

Fiddler	We do, sir, as loud as we can possibly.	
Shakestone	Play out, that we may hear you.	
Fiddler	So we do sir, as loud as we can possibly.	
Doughty	Do you hear anything?	
All	Nothing, not we, sir.	150
Doughty	'Tis so, the rogues are bribed to cross me, and their fiddles shall suffer: I will break 'em as small as the bride-cake was today.	

[The fiddlers begin to smash their instruments]

Arthur	Look you, sir, they'll save you a labour: they are doing it themselves.	
Whetstone	Oh, brave fiddlers! There was never better scuffling for the Tutbury bull.	
Moll	[aside] This is Mother Johnson and Goody Dickinson's roguery. I find it but I cannot help it, yet I will have music. – Sir, there's a piper without, would be glad to earn money.	160
Whetstone	She has spoke to purpose, and whether this were witchcraft or not, I have heard my aunt say twenty times that no witchcraft can take hold of a	

Lancashire bagpipe, for itself is able to charm the
devil. I'll fetch him. [*Exit*]

Doughty   Well said; a good boy now. Come bride and
bridegroom, leave your kissing and fooling, and
prepare to come into the dance. We'll have a
hornpipe, and then a posset and to bed when you   170
please.

[*Enter* WHETSTONE *with a piper*]

Welcome, piper. Blow till thy bag crack again, a
lusty hornpipe, and all into the dance – nay, young
and old.

[*Piper plays and all join in the*] dance [*in which*]
LAWRENCE *and* PARNELL *reel. At the end,*
MOLL *and the piper* [*vanish*]

All   Bravely performed.

Doughty   Stay, where's my lass?

Arthur, Bantam,
& Shakestone   Vanished! She and the piper both vanished,
nobody knows how.

Doughty   Now do I plainly perceive again: here has been
nothing but witchery all this day. Therefore, in to   180
your posset and agree among yourselves as you
can. I'll out o' the house, and gentlemen, if you
love me or yourselves, follow me.

Arthur, Bantam,
Shakestone, & Whetstone   Ay, ay, away, away!   *Exeunt*

Seely   Now, good son, wife, and daughter, let me entreat

	you be not angry.	
Winny	Oh, you are a trim mother, are you not?	
Joan	Indeed, child; I'll do so no more.	
Gregory	[*To* LAWRENCE] Now, sir, I'll talk with you, your champions are all gone.	190
Lawrence	Well, sir, and what wi' you do then?	
Parnell	Why, why, what's here to do? Come away, and quickly, and see us into our bride-chamber, and delicately lodged together, or we'll whip you out o' doors i'th' morn to sojourn in the common! Come away.	
All	We follow ye. *Exeunt*	

ACT 4, SCENE 1

Enter MISTRESS GENEROUS [*carrying a bridle*]
and ROBERT

Mrs Generous	Know you this jingling bridle, if you see't again? I wanted but a pair of jingling spurs to make you mend your pace and put you into a sweat.
Robert	Yes, I have reason to know it after my hard journey. They say there be light women, but for your own part, though you be merry, yet I may be sorry for your heaviness.
Mrs Generous	I see thou art not quite tired by shaking of thyself. 'Tis a sign that as thou hast brought me hither, so thou art able to bear me back, and so you are like good Robert. You will not let me have your master's gelding, you will not? Well, sir, as you like this journey, so deny him to me hereafter.
Robert	You say well; mistress, you have jaded me. A pox take you for a jade, now I bethink myself how damnably did I ride last night, and how devilishly have I been rid now.
Mrs Generous	Do you grumble, you groom? Now the bridle's off, I turn thee to grazing. Gramercy, my good horse. I have no better provender for thee at this time; thou hadst best like Aesop's ass to feed upon thistles, of which this place will afford thee plenty. I am bid to a better banquet, which done, I'll take thee up from grass, spur Cut, and make a short-

10

20

	cut home. Farewell.
Robert	A pox upon your tail!

Enter all the witches and MOLL, *at several doors*

Witches	The lady of the feast is come. Welcome, welcome.
Mrs Generous	Is all the cheer that was prepar'd to grace The wedding feast yet come?
Gillian	Part of it's here.

                    The other we must pull for.
                              [*Observing Robert*] But what's he?   30

Mrs Generous	My horse, my horse, ha, ha, ha!
Witches	Ha, ha, ha! *Exeunt*

Robert   'My horse, my horse'! I would I were now some
country major and in authority, to see if I would
not venture to rouse your satanical sisterhood. [*He
walks around the stage*] 'Horse, horse, see thou be,
and where I point thee, carry me': is that the trick
on't? The devil himself shall be her carrier next if
I can shun her, and yet my master will not believe
there's any witches. There's no running away, for
I neither know how nor whither. Besides, to my   40
thinking there's a deep ditch and a high quick-set
about me.

[*Enter* MISTRESS GENEROUS, MOLL,
GILLIAN, MEG, MAWD, *and* BOY. *A table
holding the remains of a feast is brought in, and ropes
hang from above*]

How shall I pass the time? [*He peers around a stage-post*] What place is this? It looks like an old barn. I'll peep in at some cranny or other, and try if I can see what they are doing. Such a bevy of beldams did I never behold, and cramming like so many cormorants. Marry, choke you with a mischief!   50

Gillian   Whoop! Whurr! Here's a stir,
Never a cat, never a cur,
But that we must have this demur.

Moll   A second course!

Mrs Generous   Pull, and pull hard,
For all that hath lately been prepar'd

[*The witches pull on the ropes*]

For the great wedding feast.

Moll   As chief,
Of Doughty's sirloin of roast beef.

All the witches   Ha, ha, ha!

[*A joint of meat from above lands in a dish on the table*]

Meg   'Tis come, 'tis come!   60
Mawd   Where hath it all this while been?

Meg   Some
Delay hath kept it, now 'tis here,
For bottles next of wine and beer,
The merchants' cellars they shall pay for't.

[*Bottles from above land on the table*]

Mrs Generous   Well,
What sod or roast meat more, pray tell?

| Gillian | Pull for the poultry, fowl, and fish, |
| | For empty shall not be a dish. |

[More meats come from above]

| Robert | [*aside*] A pox take them; must only they feed upon |
| | hot meat, and I upon nothing but cold salads? |

| Mrs Generous | This meat is tedious; now some fairy   70 |
| | Fetch what belongs unto the dairy. |

[Plates and vessels come from above]

| Moll | That's butter, milk, whey, curds, and cheese; |
| | We nothing by the bargain leese. |

| All the witches | Ha, ha, ha! |

| Gillian | Boy, there's meat for you. |

| Boy | Thank you. |

| Gillian | And drink, too. |

| Meg | What beast was by thee hither rid? |

| Mawd | A badger nab. |

| Meg | And I bestrid |
| | A porcupine that never prick'd.   80 |

| Moll | The dull sides of a bear I kick'd. |
| | I know how you rid, Lady Nan. |

| Mrs Generous | Ha, ha, ha! Upon the knave my man. |

| Robert | [*aside*] A murrain take you; I am sure my hooves |
| | paid for't. |

Boy	[*Putting down the food and drink given him*] Meat,
	lie there, for thou hast no taste, and drink there,
	for thou hast no relish, for in neither of them is

there either salt or savour.

All the witches   Pull for the posset, pull!   90

Robert   The bride's posset, on my life. Nay, if they come
                  to their spoon meat once, I hope they'll break up
                  their feast presently.

Mrs Generous   So those that are our waiters near,
                  Take hence this wedding cheer.
                  We will be lively all, and make this barn our hall.

                  [*Enter several spirits who clear away the banquet*]

Gillian   You, our familiars, come.
                  In speech let all be dumb,
                  And to close up our feast,
                  To welcome every guest,   100
                  A merry round let's dance.

Meg   Some music, then, i'th' air,
                  Whilst thus by pair and pair
                  We nimbly foot it. Strike! (*Music [plays from above]*)

Moll   We are obey'd.

A spirit   And we hell's ministers shall lend our aid.

                  [*Each witch dances with her familiar spirit, singing a
                  song*]

Mawd   Come Mawsy, come Puckling,

Moll   And come, my sweet suckling,

Meg   My pretty Mamilion, my joy.

All the witches Fall each to his duggy,   110
                  While kindly we huggy

	As tender as nurse over boy.	
	Then suck our bloods freely	
	And with it be jolly,	
	While merrily we sing, hey trolly lolly.	

| *Mawd* | We'll dandle and clip ye, |

| *Moll* | We'll stroke ye, and leap ye, |

| *Meg* | And all that we have is your due. |

All the witches	The feats you do for us,	
	And those which you store us	120
	Withal, ties us only to you.	
	Then suck our bloods freely	
	And with it be jolly,	
	While merrily we sing, hey trolly lolly.	

[*While they sing, the* BOY *speaks*]

| *Boy* | [*aside*] Now, whilst they are in their jollity and do not mind me, I'll steal away and shift for myself, though I lose my life for't. | *Exit* |

Meg	Enough, enough. Now part	
	To see the bride's vex'd heart,	
	The bridegroom's too and all,	130
	That vomit up their gall	
	For lack o'th' wedding cheer.	

| *Gillian* | But stay, where's the boy? Look out, if he escape us we are all betrayed. |

[*The witches chase after the* BOY, *as far as the door*]

| *Meg* | No following further; yonder horsemen come. In vain is our pursuit. Let's break up court. |

Gillian	Where shall we next meet?
Mawd	At mill.
Meg	But when?
Mrs Generous	At night.
Meg	To horse, to horse! Where's my Mamilion?
Mawd	And my incubus?
Gillian	My tiger to bestride?
Moll	My puggy?
Mrs Generous	My horse?
All the witches	Away, away! 140 The night we have feasted, now comes on the day.

ROBERT *stands amazed* [*as* MEG, MAWD,
GILLIAN, *and* MOLL *each mount a spirit*]

Mrs Generous	[*To* ROBERT] Come, sirrah, stoop your head like a tame jade. Whilst I put on your bridle.
Robert	I pray, Mistress, ride me as you would be rid.
Mrs Generous	That's at full speed.
Robert	[*aside*] Nay, then, I'll try conclusions. [*He snatches the bridle and puts on her*] 'Mare, mare, see thou be, And where I point thee carry me.'

A great noise within at their parting. Exeunt.

A Spell?

[4.2]   Scene 2

Enter GENEROUS, *making himself ready*
[*for a journey*]

Generous   I see what man is loath to entertain
                  Offers itself to him most frequently,
                  And that which we most covet to embrace
                  Doth seldom court us and proves most averse.
                  For I, that never could conceive a thought
                  Of this my woman worthy a rebuke
                  (As one that in her youth bore her so fairly
                  That she was taken for a seeming saint),
                  To render me such just occasion
                  That I should now distrust her in her age –   10
                  'Distrust'? I cannot: that would bring me in
                  The poor aspersion of fond jealousy,
                  Which even from our first meeting I abhorr'd.
                  The genteel fashion sometimes we observe
                  To sunder beds, but most in these hot months,
                  June, July, August; so we did last night.
                  Now I, as ever tender of her health
                  And therefore rising early as I use,
                  Ent'ring her chamber to bestow on her
                  A custom'd visit, find the pillow swelled,   20
                  Unbruis'd with any weight, the sheets unruffled,
                  The curtains neither drawn nor bed laid down,
                  Which shows she slept not in my house tonight.
                  Should there be any contract betwixt her
                  And this my groom to abuse my honest trust,
                  I should not take it well. But for all this,
                  Yet cannot I be jealous. [*He calls*] Robin!

                  Enter ROBERT

Generous	Is my horse safe, lusty, and in good plight?
	What, feeds he well?
Robert	Yes, sir, he's broad buttock'd
	And full flank'd; he doth not bate an ace of his flesh. 30
Generous	When was he rid last?
Robert	Not, sir, since you back'd him.
Generous	Sirrah, take heed I find you not a knave!
	Have you not lent him to your mistress late?
	So late as this last night?
Robert	Who, I, sir?
	May I die, sir, if you find me in a lie, sir!
Generous	Then I shall find him where I left him last?
Robert	No doubt, sir.
Generous	Give me the key o'th' stable.
Robert	[*He hands over the key*] There, sir.
Generous	Sirrah, your mistress was abroad all night,
	Nor is she yet come home. If there I find him not, 40
	I shall find thee what to this present hour
	I never did suspect, and, I must tell thee,
	Will not be to thy profit. *Exit*
Robert	Well, sir, find what you can, him you shall find.
	And what you find else, it may be for that, instead
	of 'gramercy horse' you may say 'gramercy
	Robin'. You will believe there are no witches! Had
	I not been late bridled I could have said more, but
	I hope she is tied to the rack that will confess
	something, and though not so much as I know, 50

yet no more than I dare justify –

Enter GENEROUS

Have you found your gelding, sir?

Generous	Yes, I have.
Robert	I hope not spurred, nor put into a sweat. You may see by his plump belly and sleek legs, he hath not been sore travailed.
Generous	You're a saucy groom to receive horses Into my stable and not ask me leave. Is't for my profit to buy hay and oats For every stranger's jades?
Robert	I hope, sir, you find none feeding there but your own. If there be any you suspect, they have nothing to champ on but the bridle.
Generous	Sirrah, whose jade is that tied to the rack?
Robert	The mare you mean, sir?
Generous	Yes, that old mare.
Robert	Old, do you call her? You shall find the mark Still in her mouth when the bridle is out of it! I can assure you 'tis your own beast.
Generous	A beast thou art to tell me so. Hath the wine Not yet left working, not the Mitre wine, That made thee to believe witchcraft? Prithee, Persuade me to be a drunken sot Like to thyself, and not to know mine own.
Robert	I'll not persuade you to anything. You will believe nothing but what you see. I say the beast is your

60

70

own, and you have most right to keep her. She
hath cost you more the currying than all the
combs in your stable are worth. You have paid for
her provender this twenty years and upwards, and
furnished her with all the caparisons that she hath
worn, of my knowledge. And because she hath   80
been ridden hard the last night, do you now
renounce her?

Generous   Sirrah, I fear some stolen jade of your own
That you would have me keep.

Robert   I am sure I found her no jade the last time I rid
her. She carried me the best part of a hundred
miles in less than a quarter of an hour.

Generous   The devil she did!

Robert   Yes, so I say, either the devil or she did. An't
please you walk in and take off her bridle, and   90
then tell me who hath more right to her, you or I.

Generous   Well, Robert, for this once I'll play the groom
And do your office for you.   *Exit*

Robert   I pray do, sir, but take heed lest when the bridle is
out of her mouth, she put it not into yours. If she
do, you are a gone man if she but say once
'Horse, horse, see thou be'. Be you rid, if you
please, for me.

                   Enter GENEROUS *and* MISTRESS
                   GENEROUS, *he with a bridle*

Generous   My blood is turn'd to ice, and all my vitals
Have ceas'd their working! Dull stupidity   100

Surpriseth me at once and hath arrested
That vigorous agitation which till now
Express'd a life within me. I, methinks,
Am a mere marble statue and no man.
Unweave my age, O Time, to my first thread;
Let me lose fifty years in ignorance spent,
That being made an infant once again
I may begin to know what, or where, am I
To be thus lost in wonder.

Mrs Generous	Sir –	110
Generous	Amazement still pursues me: how am I chang'd,	
	Or brought ere I can understand myself	
	Into this new world?	
Robert	You will believe no witches?	
Generous	This makes me believe all, ay anything,	
	And that myself am nothing. Prithee, Robin,	
	Lay me to myself open: what art thou,	
	Or this new transform'd creature?	
Robert	I am Robin, and this your wife, my mistress.	
Generous	Tell me the Earth	120
	Shall leave its seat and mount to kiss the moon,	
	Or that the moon, enamour'd of the Earth,	
	Shall leave her sphere to stoop to us thus low.	
	What? What's this in my hand, that at an instant	
	Can from a four-legged creature make a thing	
	So like a wife?	
Robert	A bridle, a jingling bridle, sir.	
Generous	A bridle? Hence enchantment!	

[*He*] *casts it away.* ROBERT *takes it up*

	A viper were more safe within my hand	
	Than this charm'd engine.	130

Robert   Take heed, sir, what you do. If you cast it hence
and she catch it up, we that are here now may be
rid as far as the Indies within these few hours.
[*To* MISTRESS GENEROUS] Mistress, down
on your mare's bones, or your marrowbones,
whether you please, and confess yourself to be
what you are: and that's, in plain English, a witch,
a grand, notorious, witch!

Generous   A witch? My wife a witch?

Robert   So it appears by the story.   140

Generous   The more I strive to unwind
Myself from this meander, I the more
Therein am intricated. Prithee, woman,
Art thou a witch?

Mrs Generous   It cannot be denied,
I am such a curs'd creature.

Generous   Keep aloof,
And do not come too near me! Oh my trust,
Have I, since first I understood myself,
Been of my soul so chary (still to study
What best was for its health, to renounce all
The works of that black fiend with my best force)   150
And hath that serpent twin'd me so about
That I must lie so often and so long
With a devil in my bosom?

Mrs Generous   Pardon, sir –

Generous   'Pardon'? Can such a thing as that be hop'd?
Lift up thine eyes, lost woman, to yon hills;

	It must be thence expected. Look not down
	Unto that horrid dwelling which thou hast sought
	At such dear rate to purchase. Prithee, tell me,
	For now I can believe, art thou a witch? 160
Mrs Generous	I am.
Generous	With that word I am thunderstuck
	And know not what to answer. Yet resolve me,
	Hast thou made any contract with that fiend,
	The enemy of mankind?
Mrs Generous	Oh, I have.
Generous	What, and how far?
Mrs Generous	I have promis'd him my soul.
Generous	Ten thousand times better thy body had
	Been promis'd to the stake, ay and mine too,
	To have suffer'd with thee in a hedge of flames,
	Than such a compact ever had been made. Oh –
Robert	What cheer, sir? Show yourself a man, though 170
	she appeared so late a beast. Mistress, confess all:
	better here than in a worse place. Out with it!
Generous	Resolve me, how far doth that contract stretch?
Mrs Generous	What interest in this soul myself could claim,
	I freely gave him, but his part that made it,
	I still reserve, not being mine to give.
Generous	Oh, cunning devil! Foolish woman, know
	Where he can claim but the least little part
	He will usurp the whole. Thou'rt a lost woman.
Mrs Generous	I hope not so.
Generous	Why, hast thou any hope? 180

Mrs Generous	Yes, sir, I have.
Generous	Make it appear to me.
Mrs Generous	I hope I never bargain'd for that fire Further than penitent tears have power to quench.
Generous	I would see some of them!
Mrs Generous	You behold them now, If you look on me with charitable eyes, Tinctur'd in blood, blood issuing from the heart. Sir, I am sorry. When I look towards heaven I beg a gracious pardon; when on you, Methinks your native goodness should not be Less pitiful than they. 'Gainst both I have err'd; From both I beg atonement.
Generous	May I presume't?
Mrs Generous	I kneel to both your mercies. [*She kneels, crying*]
Generous	Know'st thou what a witch is?
Mrs Generous	Alas, none better, Or after mature recollection can be More sad to think on't.
Generous	Tell me, are those tears As full of true-hearted penitence As mine of sorrow, to behold what state, What desperate state, thou'rt fall'n in?
Mrs Generous	Sir, they are.
Generous	Rise, and as I do, so heaven pardon me. We all offend, but from such falling off Defend us. [*She rises*] Well, I do remember wife, When I first took thee 'twas for good and bad.

190

200

Oh, change thy bad to good that I may keep thee,
As then we passed our faiths, till death us sever.
I will not aggravate thy grief too much
By needless iteration. Robin, hereafter
Forget thou hast a tongue: if the least syllable
Of what hath pass'd be rumour'd, you lose me,
But if I find you faithful, you gain me ever.

Robert A match, sir: you shall find me as mute as   210
    If I had the bridle still in my mouth.

Generous Oh, woman, thou hadst need to weep thyself
    Into a fountain, such a penitent spring
    As may have power to quench invisible flames
    In which my eyes shall aid. Too little, all;
    If not too little, all's forgiven, forgot.
    Only thus much remember: thou hadst extermin'd
    Thyself out of the bless'd society
    Of saints and angels, but on thy repentance
    I take thee to my bosom, once again   220
    My wife, sister, and daughter.
       [*To* ROBERT] Saddle my gelding;
    Some business that may hold me for two days
    Calls me aside.

    [*Exeunt* GENEROUS *and* MISTRESS GENEROUS]

Robert I shall, sir! Well, now my mistress hath promised
    to give over her witchery, I hope, though I still
    continue her man, yet she will make me no more
    her journey-man. To prevent which, the first
    thing I do shall be to burn the bridle, and then
    away with the witch.   *Exit*

[4.3]

Scene 3

Enter ARTHUR and DOUGHTY

Arthur	Sir, you have done a right noble courtesy, which deserves a memory as long as the name of friendship can bear mention.
Doughty	What I have done, I ha' done. If it be well, 'tis well. I do not like the bouncing of good offices. If the little care I have taken shall do these poor people good, I have my end in't, and so my reward.

Enter BANTAM

Bantam	Now, gentlemen, you seem very serious.
Arthur	'Tis true we are so, but you are welcome to the knowledge of our affairs.
Bantam	How does thine uncle and aunt, Gregory and his sister, the families of Seelys, agree yet? Can you tell?
Arthur	That is the business: the Seely household is divided now.
Bantam	How so, I pray?
Arthur	You know, and cannot but with pity know, Their miserable condition: how The good old couple were abus'd, and how The young abus'd themselves. If we may say That any of 'em are their selves at all, Which sure we cannot, nor approve them fit To be their own disposers, that would give

10

20

	The governance of such a house and living
	Into their vassals' hands, to thrust them out on't
	Without or law or order. This consider'd,
	This gentleman and myself have taken home,
	By fair entreaty, the old folks to his house,
	The young to mine, until some wholesome order 30
	By the judicious of the commonwealth
	Shall for their persons and estate be taken.
Bantam	But what becomes of Lawrence and his Parnell,
	The lusty couple? What do they now?
Doughty	Alas, poor folks, they are as far to seek of how they
	do, or what they do, or what they should do, as
	any of the rest. They are all grown idiots, and till
	some of these damnable jades with their devilish
	devices be found out to discharm them, no
	remedy can be found. I mean to lay the country 40
	for their hagships, and, if I can anticipate the
	purpose of their grand Master Devil, to confound
	'em before their lease be out. Be sure I'll do't.
(Cry within)	'A skimmington, a skimmington, a skimmington!'
Doughty	What's the matter now! Is hell broke loose?

Enter SHAKESTONE

Arthur	Tom Shakestone! How now, canst tell the news?
Shakestone	The news? Ye hear it up i'th'air, do you not?
(Cry within)	'A skimmington, a skimmington, a skimmington!'
Shakestone	Hark ye, do you not hear it? There's a
	skimmington towards, gentlemen. 50

Doughty	Ware wedlock, ho!
Bantam	At whose suit, I prithee, is Don Skimmington come to town?
Shakestone	I'll tell you, gentlemen. [*To* DOUGHTY *and* ARTHUR] Since you have taken home old Seely and his wife to your house, and you their son and daughter to yours, the housekeepers Lawrence and his late bride Parnell are fallen out by themselves.
Arthur	How, prithee?
Shakestone	The quarrel began, they say, upon the wedding night and in the bride bed.
Bantam	For want of bedstaves?
Shakestone	No, but a better implement, it seems, the bridegroom was unprovided of, a homely tale to tell. → *Could not perform.*
Doughty	Now, out upon her, she has a greedy worm in her! I have heard the fellow complained on for an over-mickle man among the maids.
Arthur	Is his haste to go to bed at afternoon come to this now?
Doughty	Witchery, witchery, more witchery! Still flat and plain witchery! Now do I think upon the codpiece point the young jade gave him at the wedding. She is a witch, and that was a charm, if there be any in the world.
Arthur	A ligatory point.
Bantam	Alas, poor Lawrence.
Shakestone	[*To* DOUGHTY *and* ARTHUR] He's coming to

60

70

	make his moan to you about it, and she, too. Since you have taken their masters and mistresses to your care, you must do them right too.	80
Doughty	Marry, but I'll not undertake her at these years, if lusty Lawrence cannot do't!	
Bantam	But has she beaten him?	
Shakestone	Grievously broke his head in I know not how many places, of which the hoydens have taken notice and will have a skimmington on horse-back presently. Look ye, here comes both plaintiff and defendant.	

Enter LAWRENCE AND PARNELL

Doughty	How now, Lawrence. What, hast thy wedlock brought thee already to thy night-cap?	90
Lawrence	Yea, God wot, sir. I were wedded but all too soon.	
Parnell	Ha' you reason to complain or I, trow you, Gaffer Do-Nought? Woe worth the day that ever I wedded a Do-Nought!	
Arthur, Bantam, & Shakestone	Nay, hold, Parnell, hold!	
Doughty	We have heard enough of your valour already. We know you have beaten him; let that suffice.	
Parnell	Were ever poor maiden betrayed as I were unto a swag-bellied churl, that cannot, aw, aw, that cannot –	100
Lawrence	What says she?	
Doughty	I know not. She caterwauls, I think. Parnell, be	

	patient, good Parnell, and a little modest too; 'tis not amiss. We know not the relish of every ear that hears us; let's talk within ourselves. What's the defect? What's the impediment? Lawrence has had a lusty name among the bachelors.
Parnell	What he were when he were a bachelor, I know better than the best maid i'th' town. I would I had not.
Arthur, Bantam, & Shakestone	Peace, Parnell!
Parnell	'Twere that that cozened me. He has not now as he had then!
Arthur, Bantam, & Shakestone	Peace, good Parnell!
Parnell	For then he could, but now he cannot, he cannot.
Arthur, Bantam, & Shakestone	Fie, Parnell, fie!
Parnell	I say again and again, he cannot, he cannot.
Arthur, Bantam, & Shakestone	Alas, poor Parnell!
Parnell	I am not a bit the better for him sin' we were wed. ([*She*] *cries*)
Doughty	Here's good stuff for a jury of women to pass upon.
Arthur	But Parnell, why have you beaten him so grievously? What would you have him do in this case?
Doughty	[*aside*] He's out of a doing case, it seems!

Line numbers: 110, 120

| Parnell | Marry, sir, and beat him will I into his grave, or back to the priest, and be unwedded again, for I wi' not be bound to lie with him, and live with him the life of an honest woman, for all the life's good in Lancashire. | 130 |

| Doughty | 'An honest woman', that's a good mind, Parnell. What say you to this, Lawrence? |

| Lawrence | Keep her off o' me, and I sha' tell you. An she be by I am nobody. But keep her off and search me, let me be searched as never witch was searched, and find anything more or less upo' me than a sufficient man should have, and let me be hanged by't. | 140 |

| Arthur | Do you hear this, Parnell? |

| Parnell | Ah, liar, liar, de'il take the liar. Truss ye and hang ye! |

| Doughty | Alas, it is too plain: the poor fellow is bewitched. Here's a plain *maleficium versus hanc* now. |

| Arthur | And so is she bewitched too into this immodesty. |

| Bantam | She would never talk so else. |

| Lawrence | I pray you, gi' me the lere o' that Latin, sir. |

| Doughty | The meaning is, you must get half a dozen bastards within this twelvemonth, and that will mend your next marriage. | 150 |

| Lawrence | An I thought it would ma' Parnell love me, I'd be sure on't and go about it now right. |

| Shakestone | You're soon provided, it seems, for such a journey. |

| Doughty | Best tarry till thy head be whole, Lawrence. |

Parnell	Nay, nay, nay, I's quite casten away an't I be unwedded again, and then I undertake to find three better husbands in a bean-cod.
Shakestone	Hark, gentlemen, the show is coming.
Arthur	What, shall we stay and see't?
Bantam	Oh, by all means, gentlemen.
Doughty	'Tis best to have these away first.
Parnell	Nay, marry, sha' you not sir! I hear you well enough, and I con the meaning o' the show well enough. An I stay not the show and see not the show and ma' one i' the show, let me be hanged up for a show. I'll ware them to mell or ma' with a woman that mells or ma's with a testril, a longie, a do-little losel that cannot, and if I skim not their skimmington's coxcomb for't, ma' that warplin boggle me a week longer, and that's a curse eno' for any wife, I trow.
Doughty	Agreed. Perhaps 'twill mend the sport.

160

170

> *Enter [a] drum[mer] beating before a skimmington and his wife on a horse [followed by] diverse country rustics. As they pass,* PARNELL *pulls [the] skimmington off the horse and* LAWRENCE *[likewise the] skimmington's wife, [and] they beat them. [The] drum[mer] beats [an] alarm [and the] horse comes away. The hoydens at first oppose the gentlemen, who draw [their swords, at which] the clowns vail bonnet. [They all] make a ring [while]* PARNELL *and [the] skim[mington] fight.*

Doughty	Beat, drum, alarum! Enough, enough, here my

masters! [PARNELL *drops the skimmington*]
[*To the* RABBLE *of hoydens*] Now patch up your
show if you can, and catch your horse again. And
when you have done, drink that. [*He gives them
money*]

Rabble	Thank your worship.	*Exeunt* [*with a*] *shout*
Parnell	Let them, as they like this, gang a procession with their idol skimmington again.	180
Arthur	Parnell, thou didst bravely.	
Parnell	I am sure I ha' drawn blood o' their idol.	
Lawrence	And I think I tickled his wife.	
Parnell	Yea, to be sure, you be one of the old ticklers! But with what, can you tell?	
Lawrence	Yea, with her own ladle.	
Parnell	Yea, marry, a ladle is something!	
Doughty	Come, you have both done well. Go into my house, see your old master and mistress, while I travel a course to make ye all well again. I will now a-witch-hunting.	190
Parnell	No course for us but to be unwedded again.	
Arthur, Bantam, & Shakestone	We are for Whetstone and his aunt, you know.	
Doughty	Farewell, farewell.	

Exeunt [DOUGHTY, PARNELL, *and*
LAWRENCE *through one door, and* ARTHUR,
BANTAM, *and* SHAKESTONE *through the other*]

Scene 4

[4.4]

Enter MISTRESS GENEROUS *and* MOLL

Mrs Generous	Welcome, welcome, my girl. What, hath thy puggy Yet suck'd upon thy pretty duggy?
Moll	All's well at home and abroad too. What e'er I bid my pug, he'll do. You sent for me?
Mrs Generous	I did.
Moll	And why?
Mrs Generous	Wench, I'll tell thee, thou and I Will walk a little. How doth Meg, And her Mamilion?
Moll	Of one leg She's grown lame.
Mrs Generous	Because the beast Did miss us last Good Friday feast, 10 I guessed as much.
Moll	But All Saints' night She met, though she did halt downright.
Mrs Generous	Dickinson and Hargreave, prithee tell, How do they?
Moll	All about us well. But puggy whisper'd in mine ear That you of late were put in fear.
Mrs Generous	The slave, my man.

Moll	Who, Robin?
Mrs Generous	He,
Moll	My sweetheart?
Mrs Generous	Such a trick serv'd me.
Moll	About the bridle, now alack!
Mrs Generous	The villain brought me to the rack. 20
	Tied was I both to rack and manger.
Moll	But thence how 'scap'd you?
Mrs Generous	Without danger,
	I thank my spirit.
Moll	Ay, but then
	How pacified was your good man?
Mrs Generous	Some passionate words mix'd with forc'd tears
	Did so enchant his eyes and ears,
	I made my peace, with promise never
	To do the like. But once and ever
	A witch, thou knowst. Now, understand,
	New business we took in hand. 30
	My husband pack'd out of the town,
	Know that the house and all's our own.

Enter WHETSTONE

Whetstone	Naunt, is this your promise, Naunt? What, Moll! How dost thou, Moll? [*To* MISTRESS GENEROUS] You told me you would put a trick upon these gentlemen, whom you made me invite to supper, who abused and called me bastard. [*aside to* MOLL] And when shall I get one upon

thee, my sweet rogue? – And that you would do I
know not what, for you would not tell me what   40
you would do. [*aside to* MOLL] And shall you and
I never have any doing together? – Supper is done
and the table ready to withdraw, and I am risen
the earliest from the board, and yet for ought I can
see I am never a whit the nearer.
[*aside to* MOLL] What, not one kiss at parting, Moll?

Mrs Generous   Well, cousin, this is all you have to do:
Retire the gallants to some private room,
Where call for wine and junkets, what you please,
Then thou shalt need to do no other thing   50
Than what this note directs thee.
          [*She hands him a paper*] Observe that,
And trouble me no farther.

Whetstone   Very good!
I like this beginning well, for where they slighted
me before, they shall find me a man of note.   *Exit*

Moll   Of this, the meaning?

Mrs Generous   Marry, lass,
To bring a new conceit to pass.
Thy spirit I must borrow more,
To fill the number three or four,
Whom we will use to no great harm,
Only assist me with thy charm.   60
This night we'll celebrate to sport:
'Tis all for mirth, we mean no hurt.

Moll   My spirit and myself command,
Mamilion and the rest at hand
Shall all assist.

| Mrs Generous | Withdraw then quick, | |
| | Now, gallants, there's for you a trick. | *Exeunt* |

[4.5]

Enter WHETSTONE, ARTHUR,
SHAKESTONE [*and*] BANTAM

| Whetstone | Here's a more private room, gentlemen, free from the noise of the hall. Here we may talk, and throw the chamber out the casements. [*He calls to servants within*] Some wine and a short banquet! |

Enter [*servants*] *with a banquet, wine, and two tapers*

Whetstone	So now leave us.	[*Exit servants*]
Arthur	We are much bound to you, Master Whetstone, For this great entertainment. I see you command The house in the absence of your uncle.	
Whetstone	Yes, I thank my aunt, for though I be but a daily guest, yet I can be welcome to her at midnight.	10
Shakestone	How shall we pass the time?	
Bantam	In some discourse.	
Whetstone	But no such discourse as we had last, I beseech you.	
Bantam	Now, Master Whetstone, you reflect on me. 'Tis true, at our last meeting some few words Then passed my lips which I could wish forgot. I think I call'd you 'bastard'.	
Whetstone	I think so too. But what's that amongst friends? For I would fain	

	know which amongst you all knows his own father. 20
Bantam	You are merry with your friends, Master By-blow, and we are guests here in your uncle's house and therefore privileged.

Enter [*unseen*] MISTRESS GENEROUS, MOLL,
and spirits

Whetstone	I presume you had no more privilege in your getting than I. But tell me, gentlemen, is there any man here amongst you that hath a mind to see his father?
Bantam	Why? Who shall show him?
Whetstone	That's all one. If any man here desire it, let him but speak the word and 'tis sufficient. 30
Bantam	Why, I would see my father.
Mrs Generous	Strike! (*Music* [*plays*])

Enter [*a spirit like*] *a pedant dancing to the music. The*
strain done, he points at BANTAM *and looks full in his*
face.

Whetstone	Do you know him that looks so full in your face?
Bantam	Yes, well: a pedant in my father's house, Who, being young, taught me my A, B, C.
Whetstone	In his house that goes for your father, you would say. For, know, one morning when your mother's husband rid early to have a *Nisi prius* tried at Lancaster 'sizes, he crept into his warm place, lay

	close by her side, and then were you got. Then, come, your heels and tail together, and kneel unto your own dear father.	40
Arthur, Shakestone & Whetstone	Ha, ha, ha!	
Bantam	I am abused!	
Whetstone	Why laugh you, gentlemen? It may be more men's cases than his or mine.	
Bantam	To be thus jeer'd!	
Arthur	Come, take it as a jest, For I presume 'twas meant no otherwise.	
Whetstone	Would either of you two now see his father in earnest?	50
Shakestone	Yes, canst thou show me mine?	
Mrs Generous	Strike! *[Music plays]*	

Enter [a spirit like] a nimble tailor, dancing. [The strain done, he points at SHAKESTONE and looks full in his face.]

Whetstone	He looks on you! Speak, do you know him?	
Shakestone	Yes, he was my mother's tailor. I remember him ever since I was a child.	
Whetstone	Who, when he came to take measure of her upper parts, had more mind to the lower. Whilst the good man was in the fields hunting, he was at home whoring. Then, since no better comfort can be had.	60

Come down, come down, ask blessing of your dad.

Arthur &
Whetstone   Ha, ha, ha!

Bantam   This cannot be endur'd!

Arthur   It is plain witchcraft.
Nay, since we all are bid unto one feast,
Let's fare alike: come, show me mine too.

Mrs Generous   Strike!   [*Music plays*]

        Enter ROBERT *with a switch and a curry-comb,*
        [*dancing. The strain done,*] *he points at* ARTHUR
                [*and looks full in his face*].

Whetstone   He points at you.

Arthur   What then?

Whetstone   You know him?

Arthur   Yes,
Robin, the groom belonging to this house.

Whetstone   And never served your father?

Arthur   In's youth I think he did.   70

Whetstone   Who, when your supposed father had business at
the Lord President's court in York, stood for his
attorney at home, and so it seems you were got by
deputy. What, all amort? If you will have but a
little patience, stay and you shall see mine, too.
And know I show you him the rather,
To find who hath the best man to his father.

Mrs Generous   Strike!   [*Music plays*]

*Enter [a spirit like] a gallant, [dancing. The strain done,
he points at* WHETSTONE *and looks full in his face.]*

Whetstone   Now, gentlemen, make me your precedent.
Learn your duties and do as I do. [*He kneels to the*   80
spirit-as-gallant] A blessing, Dad.

Arthur   Come, come, let's home. We'll find some other time
When to dispute of these things –

Whetstone   Nay, gentlemen, no parting in spleen. Since we
have begun in mirth, let's not end in melancholy.
You see there are more By-blows than bear the
name. It is grown a great kindred in the kingdom.
Come, come, all friends! Let's into the cellar and
conclude our revels in a lusty health.

Shakestone   [*Struggling to raise his arms*] I fain would strike,   90
but cannot.

Bantam   Some strange fate holds me.
Arthur   Here then all anger end.
Let none be mad at what they cannot mend.

[*Exit* ARTHUR, SHAKESTONE, BANTAM,
and WHETSTONE]

Moll   Now say, what's next?

Mrs Generous   I'th' mill there lies
A soldier yet with unscratch'd eyes.
Summon the sisterhood together,
For we with all our spirits will thither.
And such a caterwauling keep,
That he in vain shall think to sleep.

Call Meg and Doll, Tib, Nab, and Jug,   100
Let none appear without her pug.
We'll try our utmost art and skill,
To fright the stout knave in the mill.   *Exeunt*

ACT 5, SCENE 1

Enter DOUGHTY, MILLER, *and* BOY [*wearing*]
a cap

Doughty   Thou art a brave boy, the honour of thy country.
           Thy statue shall be set up in brass upon the market
           cross in Lancaster. I bless the time that I answered
           at the font for thee. 'Zooks, did I ever think that a
           godson of mine should have fought hand to fist
           with the Devil!

Miller   He was ever an unhappy boy, sir, and like enough
           to grow acquainted with him; and friends may fall
           out sometimes.

Doughty   Thou art a dogged sire, and dost not know the   10
           virtue of my godson – my son now; he shall be thy
           son no longer. He and I will worry all the witches
           in Lancashire.

Miller   You were best take heed, though.

Doughty   I care not. Though we leave not above three
           untainted women in the parish, we'll do it.

Miller   Do what you please, sir, there's the boy stout
           enough to justify anything he has said. Now 'tis
           out, he should be my son still by that: though he
           was at death's door before he would reveal   20
           anything, the damnable jades had so threatened
           him. And as soon as ever he had told, he mended.

Doughty   'Tis well he did so. We will so swing them in two-

	penny halters, boy!
Miller	For my part, I have no reason to hinder anything that may root them all out. I have tasted enough of their mischief: witness my usage i'th' mill, which could be nothing but their roguery. One night in my sleep they set me astride, stark naked, atop of my mill, a bitter cold night too. 'Twas daylight 30 before I was waked, and I durst never speak of it to this hour, because I thought it impossible to be believed.
Doughty	Villainous hags!
Miller	And all last summer, my wife could not make a bit of butter.
Doughty	It would not come, would it?
Miller	No, sir, we could not make it come, though she and I both together churned almost our hearts out, and nothing would come but all ran into thin 40 waterish gear; the pigs would not drink it.
Doughty	Is't possible?
Miller	None but one, and he ran out of his wits upon't, till we bound his head and laid him asleep, but he has had a wry mouth ever since.
Doughty	That the Devil should put in their hearts to delight in such villainies! I have sought about these two days, and heard of a hundred such mischievous tricks, though none mortal, but could not find whom to mistrust for a witch till now this 50 boy, this happy boy, informs me.
Miller	And they should ne'er have been sought for me if

	their affrightments and devilish devices had not brought my boy into such a sickness. Whereupon indeed I thought good to acquaint your worship, and bring the boy unto you, being his godfather, and as you now stick not to say, his father.	
Doughty	After you; I thank you, gossip. But my boy, thou hast satisfied me in their names, and thy knowledge of the women, their turning into shapes, their dog-tricks and their horse-tricks, and their great feast in the barn (a pox take them with my sirloin, I say still). But a little more of thy combat with the Devil, I prithee. He came to thee like a boy, thou sayest, about thine own bigness?	60
Boy	Yes, sir, and he asked me where I dwelt, and what my name was.	
Doughty	Ah, rogue!	
Boy	But it was in a quarrelsome way, whereupon I was as stout, and asked him who made him an examiner.	70
Doughty	Ah, good boy.	
Miller	In that he was my son.	
Boy	He told me he would know or beat it out of me, and I told him he should not, and bid him do his worst, and to't we went.	
Doughty	In that he was my son again, ha boy? I see him at it now.	
Boy	We fought a quarter of an hour, till his sharp nails made my ears bleed.	80

Doughty	Oh, the grand Devil pare 'em!
Boy	I wondered to find him so strong in my hands, seeming but of mine own age and bigness, till I, looking down, perceived he had clubbed cloven feet, like ox feet, but his face was as young as mine.
Doughty	A pox, but by his feet he may be the club-footed horse-courser's father, for all his young looks.
Boy	But I was afraid of his feet, and ran from him towards a light that I saw, and when I came to it, it was one of the witches in white upon a bridge. 90 That scared me back again, and then met me the boy again, and he struck me and laid me for dead.
Miller	Till I, wondering at his stay, went out and found him in the trance. Since which time he has been haunted and frighted with goblins forty times, and never durst tell anything, as I said, because the hags had so threatened him, till in his sickness he revealed it to his mother.
Doughty	And she told nobody but folks on't. Well, gossip Gritty, as thou art a miller and a close thief, now 100 let us keep it as close as we may till we take 'em and see them handsomely hanged o' the way. Ha, my little cuff-devil, thou art a made man. Come, away with me.

[*Exit* MILLER *by one door and* DOUGHTY *and*
BOY *by the other*]

[5.2]   Scene 2

Enter SOLDIER

Soldier   These two nights I have slept well and heard no noise
               Of cats or rats. Most sure the fellow dreamt,
               And scratch'd himself in's sleep. I have travelled deserts,
               Beheld wolves, bears, and lions – indeed what not? –
               Of horrid shape, and shall I be afraid
               Of cats in mine own country? I can never
               Grow so mouse-hearted. It is now a calm
               And no wind stirring. I can bear no sail;
               Then best lie down to sleep. Nay, rest by me
               Good Morglay, my comrogue and bedfellow   10
               That never fail'd me yet; I know thou didst not.
               If I be wak'd, see thou be stirring too,
               Then come a Gib as big as Askapart
               We'll make him play at leap-frog.
               A brave soldier's lodging:
               The floor my bed, a millstone for my pillow,
               The sails for curtains. So, good night. (*Lies down*)

               Enter MISTRESS GENEROUS, MOLL,
               GILLIAN, MEG, *and* MAWD, *and their spirits, at*
                           several doors

Mrs Generous   Is Nab come?

Moll   Yes

Mrs Generous   Where's Jug?

Moll   On horseback yet.
               Now lighting from her broomstaff.

Mrs Generous   But where's Peg?

Moll	Enter'd the mill already.
Mrs Generous	<div align="center">Is he fast?</div> 20
Moll	As senseless as a dormouse.
Mrs	<div align="right">Then to work,</div>

To work, my pretty Laplands: pinch, here scratch,
Do that within, without we'll keep the watch.

> *The witches [exeunt]. The spirits come about [the*
> SOLDIER] *with a dreadful noise. He starts.*

Soldier   Am I in hell? Then have amongst you, devils!
    [*He swings his sword at spirits surrounding him*]
This side and that side! What, behind? Before?
I'll keep my face unscratch'd despite you all.
      [*The spirits scratch and pinch him*]
What, do you pinch in private? Claws I feel,
But can see nothing, nothing. Pinch me thus?
Have at you then, ay, and have at you still!
And still have at you!

> [*He*] *beats them off* [*and the spirits exeunt. He*] *follows*
> *them in* [*to the tiring house*] *and enters again* [*with his*
> *sword bloodied*]

One of them I have paid.   30

In leaping out o'th' hole, a foot, or ear,
Or something I have light on. What, all gone?
All quiet? Not a cat that's heard to mew?
Nay then, I'll try to take another nap,
Though I sleep with mine eyes open.   *Exit*

[5.3]

Scene 3

Enter GENEROUS *and* ROBERT

Generous   Robin, the last night that I lodg'd at home,
           My wife, if thou remember'st, lay abroad,
           But no words of that.

Robert   You have taught me silence.

Generous   I rose thus early, much before my hour,
           To take her in her bed. 'Tis yet not five;
           The sun scarce up. Those horses take and lead 'em
           Into the stable, see them rubb'd and dress'd;
           We have rid hard. Now, in the interim I
           Will step and see how my new miller fares,
           Or whether he slept better in his charge   10
           Than those which did precede him.

Robert   Sir, I shall.

Generous   But one thing more – ([*He takes*
                          ROBERT *aside and*] *whispers* [*to him*])

Enter ARTHUR

Arthur   Now from the last night's witchcraft we are freed,
           And I, that had not power to clear myself
           From base aspersion, am at liberty
           For vow'd revenge. I cannot be at peace,
           The night-spell being took off, till I have met
           With noble Master Generous, in whose search
           The best part of this morning I have spent.
           His wife now I suspect.

Robert   By your leave, sir.   20

Arthur   Oh, you're well met! Pray tell me, how long is't

	Since you were first my father?	
Robert	Be patient, I beseech you! [ARTHUR *menaces him*] What do you mean, sir?	
Arthur	But that I honour Thy master, to whose goodness I am bound, And still must remain thankful, I should prove Worse than a murderer, a mere parricide, By killing thee my father!	
Robert	I, your father? He was a man I always loved and honoured. He bred me.	30
Arthur	And you begot me! Oh, you us'd me Finely last night!	
Generous	Pray, what's the matter, sir?	
Arthur	My worthy friend, but that I honour you As one to whom I am so much oblig'd, This villain could not stir a foot from hence Till perish'd by my sword.	
Generous	How hath he wrong'd you? Be of a milder temper, I entreat. Relate what, and when done.	
Arthur	You may command me. If ask me what wrongs, know this groom pretends He hath strumpeted my mother; if when: blaz'd Last night at midnight. If you ask me further, Where: in your own house, when he pointed to me As had I been his bastard.	40
Robert	I, do this? I am a horse again, if I got you.	

Master, why, master –

Generous	I know you, Master Arthur, for a gentleman

Of fair endowments, a most solid brain,
And settled understanding. Why, this fellow
These two day was scarce sunder'd from my side,
And for the last night, I am most assur'd   50
He slept within my chamber, twelve miles off.
We have ne'er parted since.

Arthur   You tell me wonders,
Since all your words to me are oracles,
And such as I most constantly believe.
But, sir, shall I be bold and plain withal?
I am suspicious all's not well at home.
I dare proceed no farther without leave,
Yet there is something lodg'd within my breast
Which I am loath to utter.

Generous   Keep it there,
I pray do, a season. [aside] Oh, my fears! –   60
No doubt ere long my tongue may be the key
To open that your secret.
          [To ROBERT] Get you gone sir,
And do as I commanded.

Robert   I shall, sir.
[aside] 'Father', quoth he?
I should be proud indeed of such a son.   Exit

Generous   Please you now walk with me to my mill. I fain
would see how my bold soldier speeds. It is a place
hath been much troubled. [They cross the stage]

Enter SOLDIER

Arthur	I shall wait on you. See, he appears.
Generous	Good morrow, soldier.
Soldier	A bad night I have had. 70 A murrain take your mill-sprites!
Generous	Prithee, tell me, Hast thou been frighted, then?
Soldier	How, frighted, sir! A dung-cart full of devils could not do't, But I have been so nipp'd, and pull'd, and pinch'd By a company of hell-cats.
Arthur	Fairies, sure.
Soldier	Rather foul fiends; fairies have no such claws. Yet I have kept my face whole thanks my scimitar, My trusty bilbo, but for which I vow, I had been torn to pieces. But I think I met with some of them. One, I am sure, 80 I have sent limping hence.
Generous	Didst thou fasten upon any?
Soldier	Fast or loose, most sure I made them fly And skip out of the port-holes. But the last I made her squeak; she had forgot to mew; I spoil'd her caterwauling.
Arthur	Let's see thy sword.
Soldier	To look on, not to part with from my hand; 'Tis not the soldiers' custom.
Arthur	Sir, I observe 'tis bloody towards the point.
Soldier	If all the rest 'scape scot-free, yet I am sure 90 There's one hath paid the reckoning.

| Generous | Look well about. |
| | Perhaps there may be seen some tract of blood. |

[They search and the SOLDIER] *finds the hand*

| Soldier | What's here? Is't possible cats should have hands |
| | And rings upon their fingers? |

| Arthur | Most prodigious! |

| Generous | Reach me that hand. |

| Soldier | There's that of the three I can best spare. *[He gives* |
| | *the hand to* GENEROUS] |

Generous	*[aside]* Amazement upon wonder, can this be?
	I needs must know't by most infallible marks.
	Is this the hand once plighted holy vows?
	And this the ring that bound them? Doth this last age 100
	Afford what former never durst believe?
	Oh, how have I offended those high powers
	That my great incredulity should merit
	A punishment so grievous, and to happen
	Under mine own roof, mine own bed, my bosom?

| Arthur | Know you the hand sir? |

Generous	Yes, and too well can read it.
	Good Master Arthur, bear me company
	Unto my house; in the society
	Of good men there's great solace.

| Arthur | Sir, I'll wait on you. |

| Generous | And soldier, do not leave me. Lock thy mill: 110 |
| | I have employment for thee. |

| Soldier | I shall, sir. |
| | I think I have tickled some of your tenants |

At will, that thought to revel here rent-free.
The best is, if one of the parties shall
Deny the deed, we have their hand to show.   *Exeunt*

[5.4]   Scene 5

A bed thrust out [with] MISTRESS GENEROUS *in
it. [Enter]* WHETSTONE *[and]* MOLL *[to stand]
by her*

Whetstone   Why aunt, dear aunt, honey aunt, how do you?
                 How fare you, cheer you, how is't with you? You
                 Have been been a lusty woman in your time,
                 But now you look as if you could not do
                 Withal.

Mrs Generous   Good Moll, let him not trouble me.

Moll   Fie, Master Whetstone, you keep such a noise
                 In the chamber that your aunt is desirous
                 To take a little rest and cannot.

Whetstone   In my uncle's absence, who but I should
                 Comfort my aunt. Am I not of the blood?   10
                 Am not I next of kin? Why, aunt!

Mrs Generous   Good nephew, leave me.

Whetstone   The devil shall leave you ere I'll forsake you, aunt.
                 You know, *sic* is 'so', and being so sick do you
                 think I'll leave you? [*aside*] What know I but this
                 bed may prove your death-bed, and then I hope
                 you will remember me, that is, remember me in
                 your will. – (*Knock within*) Who's that knocks with
                 such authority? Ten to one my uncle's come to
                 town.   20

Mrs Generous	If it be so, excuse my weakness to him; say I can speak with none.
Moll	I will, [*aside*] and 'scape him if I can. By this accident all must come out, and here's no stay for me. – (*Knock again*) Again! [*To* WHETSTONE] Stay you here with your aunt, and I'll go let in your uncle. [*Exit*]
Whetstone	Do, good Moll. And how, and how, sweet aunt?

Enter GENEROUS, MOLL, ARTHUR,
SOLDIER, *and* ROBERT

Generous	[*To* MOLL] You're well met here! I am told you oft frequent This house as my wife's choice companion. 30 Yet have I seldom seen you.
Moll	Pray, by your leave, sir, Your wife is taken with a sudden qualm; She hath sent me for a doctor.
Generous	But that labour I'll save you. Soldier, take her to your charge.

[SOLDIER *seizes* MOLL]

And now where's this sick woman?

Whetstone	Oh, uncle, you come in good time! My aunt is so suddenly taken as if she were ready to give up the spirit.
Generous	'Tis almost time she did! Speak, how is't wife? My nephew tells me you were took last night With a shrewd sickness, which this maid confirms. 40
Mrs Generous	Yes sir, but now desire no company.

Noise troubles me, and I would gladly sleep.

Generous   In company there's comfort. Prithee, wife,
Lend me thy hand, and let me feel thy pulse.
Perhaps some fever – by their beating I
May guess at thy disease.

Mrs Generous   My hand, 'tis there.

[GENEROUS *feels her pulse*]

Generous   A dangerous sickness and, I fear't, death.
'Tis odds you will not 'scape it. Take that back
And let me prove the t'other if perhaps
I there can find more comfort.

Mrs Generous   I pray excuse me.   50

Generous   I must not be denied. Sick folks are peevish
And must be o'errul'd, and so shall you.

Mrs Generous   Alas, I have not strength to lift it up.

Generous   If not thy hand, wife, show me but thy wrist,

[*He shows her the hand found at the mill*]

And see how this will match it. Here's a testate
That cannot be outfac'd.

Mrs Generous   I am undone.

Whetstone   Hath my aunt been playing at handy-dandy?
Nay, then, if the game go this way I fear
She'll have the worst hand on't.

Arthur   'Tis now apparent
How all the last night's business came about.   60
In this my late suspicion is confirm'd.

Generous   My heart hath bled more for thy curs'd relapse

Than drops hath issued from thy wounded arm.
But wherefore should I preach to one past hope,
Or, where the devil himself claims right in all,
Seek the least part or interest? Leave your bed!
Up, make you ready! I must deliver you
Into the hand of justice. [*To* ARTHUR] Oh, dear friend,
It is in vain to guess at this my grief,
'Tis so inundant. Soldier, take away that young –   70
But old in mischief!
And, being of these apostates rid so well,
I'll see my house no more be made a hell.
Away with them!   *Exeunt*

[5.5]   Scene 5

Enter BANTAM *and* SHAKESTONE

Bantam	I'll out o' the country, and as soon live In Lapland as Lancashire hereafter.
Shakestone	What, for a false illusive apparition? I hope the devil is not able to Persuade thee thou art a bastard?
Bantam	No, but I am afflicted to think that the devil Should have power to put such a trick upon Us, to countenance a rascal that is one.
Shakestone	I hope Arthur has taken a course with His uncle about him by this time. 10 Who would have thought such a fool as he could Have been a witch?
Bantam	Why, do you think there's any Wise folks of the quality? Can any but fools

Be drawn into a covenant with the
Greatest enemy of mankind? Yet I
Cannot think that Whetstone is the witch! The
Young quean that was at the wedding was i'th'
House, ye know.

*Enter LAWRENCE and PARNELL in their [proper]
habits*

Shakestone	See Lawrence and Parnell civilly accorded	
	Again, it seems, and accoutred as they	20
	Were wont to be when they had their wits.	

Lawrence   Blessed be the hour, I say my honey, my sweet
            Poll, that's I become thine again, and thou's
            become mine again. And may this one kiss ma'
            us two become both one for ever and a day.

Parnell   Yea, marry, Loll, and thus should it be. There is
            nought gotten by falling out; we mu' fall in or we
            get nought.

Bantam	The world's well mended here; we cannot but	
	rejoice to see this, Lawrence.	30

Lawrence   And you been welcome to it, gentlemen.

Parnell   And we been glad we ha' it for you.

Shakestone And I protest I am glad to see it.

Parnell   And thus sha' you see't till our dying hour. We've
            one love now for a lifetime. The devil sha' not ha'
            the power to put us to pieces again.

Bantam   Why, now all's right, and straight, and as it should be.

Lawrence   Yea, marry, that is it. The good hour be blessed for

it, that put the wit into my head to have a mistrust
of that pestilent cod-piece point that the wicked   40
witch Moll Spencer ga' me, ah woe worth her,
that were it that made all so nought

Bantam & Shakestone   Is't possible?

Parnell   Yea, marry, it were an enchantment, and about an
hour since it come into our hearts to do, what you
think, and we did it!

Bantam   What, Parnell?

Parnell   Marry, we take the point and we casten the point
into the fire, and the point spittered and spattered
in the fire, like an it were (love bless us) a live   50
thing in the fire, and it hopped and skipped and
wriggled and frisked in the fire, and crept about
like a worm in the fire, that it were work enough
for us both with all the chimney tools to keep it
into the fire, and it stinked in the fire, worsen than
any brimstone in the fire.

Bantam   This is wonderful as all the rest!

Lawrence   It would ha' scared any that had their wits to ha'
seen't, and we were mad only it were done.

Parnell   And this were not above an hour since, and you   60
cannot devise how we ha' loved t'one t'other by
now. You would e'en bless yourselves to see't.

Lawrence   Yea, and ha' put on our working gear, to swink
and serve our master and mistress like unto
painful servants again, as we should.

Bantam   'Tis wondrous well.

Shakestone	And are they well again?
Parnell	Yea, and well as like hea'en bless them, they are a-was well becomed as none ill had ever been anenst 'em. Lo ye, lo ye, as they come.

Enter SEELY, JOAN, GREGORY, *and* WINNY

Gregory	Sir, if a contrite heart struck through with sense	70
	Of its sharp errors, bleeding with remorse,	
	The black polluted stain it had conceived	
	Of foul unnatural disobedience,	
	May yet by your fair mercy find remission,	
	You shall upraise a son out o' the gulf	
	Of horror and despair unto a bliss	
	That shall forever crown your goodness, and	
	Instructive in my after life to serve you	
	In all the duties that befit a son.	
Seely	Enough, enough, good boy! 'Tis most apparent	80
	We all have had our errors, and as plainly	
	It now appears our judgements, yea our reason,	
	Was poison'd by some violent infection,	
	Quite contrary to nature.	
Bantam	This sounds well.	
Seely	I fear it was by witchcraft, for I now –	
	Bless'd be the power that wrought the happy means	
	Of my delivery – remember that	
	Some three months since I cross'd a weird woman	
	(One that I now suspect) for bearing with	
	A most unseemly disobedience	90
	In an untoward, ill-bred son of hers.	
	When, with an ill look and an hollow voice,	

She mutter'd out these words: 'Perhaps ere long
Thyself shalt be obedient to thy son.'
She has play'd her prank, it seems.

Gregory   Sir, I have heard
That witches apprehended under hands
Of lawful authority do lose their power,
And all their spells are instantly dissolv'd.

Seely   If it be so then at this happy hour
The witch is ta'en that over us had power.   100

[WINNY *makes obeisance to* JOAN]

Joan   Enough, child; thou art mine and all is well.

Winny   Long may you live the well-spring of my bliss,
And may my duty and my fruitful prayers
Draw a perpetual stream of blessings from you.

Seely   Gentlemen, welcome to my best friend's house.
You know the unhappy cause that drew me hither.

Bantam   And cannot but rejoice to see the remedy
So near at hand.

Enter DOUGHTY, MILLER, *and* BOY

Doughty   Come, gossip; come, boy. Gentlemen, you are
come to the bravest discovery. Master Seely and   110
the rest,how is't with you? You look reasonable
well, methinks.

Seely   Sir, we do find that we have reason enough to
thank you for your neighbourly and pious care of
us.

Doughty   Is all so well with you already? Go to, will you

know a reason for't, gentlemen? I have catched a
whole kennel of witches! [*He indicates the Seelys*]
It seems their witch is one of 'em, and so they are
discharmed; they are all in officers' hands and they   120
will touch here with two or three of them for a
little private parley before they go to the Justices.
Master Generous is coming hither too, with a
supply that you dream not of, and [*to* SEELY]
your nephew Arthur.

Bantam   You are beholden, sir, to Master Generous in
                behalf of your nephew for saving his land from
                forfeiture in time of your distraction.

Seely   I will acknowledge it most thankfully.

Shakestone   See, he comes.   130

          Enter GENEROUS, MISTRESS GENEROUS,
          ARTHUR, WHETSTONE, MOLL, SOLDIER,
                  and ROBERT

Seely   Oh, Master Generous, the noble favour you have
                showed my nephew forever binds me to you.

Generous   I pitied then your misery, and now
                Have nothing left but to bewail mine own
                In this unhappy woman.

Seely   Good Mistress Generous –

Arthur   Make a full stop there, sir! Sides, sides, make sides.
                You know her not as I do. Stand aloof there,
                mistress, with your darling witch; your nephew,
                too if you please, because though he be no witch,   140
                he is a well-willer to the infernal science.

Generous	I utterly discard him in her blood,
	And all the good that I intended him
	I will confer on this [*indicates Arthur*] virtuous gentleman.
Whetstone	Well, sir, though you be no uncle, yet mine
	Aunt's mine aunt, and shall be to her dying day.
Doughty	And that will be about a day after next 'sizes, I take
	it.

Enter [GILLIAN, MAWD, MEG], *Constable, and Officers*

	Oh, here comes more o' your naunts: naunt
	Dickinson and naunt Hargreave, 'od's fish, and 150
	your granny Johnson too! We want but a good fire
	to entertain 'em.

Witches charm together

Arthur	See how they lay their heads together?
Gillian	No succour!
Mawd	No relief!
Meg	No comfort!
Mrs Generous, Moll, *Gillian, Mawd, & Meg*	Mawsy, my Mawsy, gentle Mawsy, come!
Mawd	Come my sweet Puckling!
Meg	My Mamilion!
Arthur	What do they say?
Bantam	They call their spirits, I think.
Doughty	Now, a shame take you for a fardel of fools. Have
	you known so many of the devil's tricks and can

be ignorant of that common feat of the old juggler,   160
that is, to leave you all to the law when you are
once seized on by the talons of authority? I'll
undertake this little demigorgon constable, with
these commonwealth characters upon his staff
here, is able in spite of all your bugs-words to
stave off the grand devil for doing any of you good
till you come to his kingdom to him, and there
take what you can find.

Arthur   But gentlemen, shall we try if we can by
examination get from them something that may   170
abbreviate the cause unto the wiser in commission
for the peace before we carry them before 'em?

Generous & Seely   Let it be so.

Doughty   Well, say: stand out boy, stand out miller, stand
out Robin, stand out soldier, and lay your
accusation upon 'em.

Bantam   Speak, boy, do you know these creatures, women I
dare not call 'em?

Boy   Yes, sir, and saw them all in the barn together, and
many more, at their feast and witchery   180

Robert   And so did I, by a devilish token. I was rid thither,
though I rid home again as fast without switch or
spur.

Miller   I was ill-handled by them in the mill.

Soldier   And I sliced off a cat's foot there, that is since a
hand, whoever wants it. [Shows the hand]

Seely   How I and all my family have suffered, you all
know.

Lawrence	And how I were bewitched my Poll here knows.
Parnell	Yea, Loll, and [*indicates* MOLL] the witch I know, 190 and I prayen you gi' me but leave to scratch her well-favoury.
Bantam	Hold, Parnell.
Parnell	You can blame no honest woman, I trow, To scratch for the thing she loves.
Moll	Ha, ha, ha!
Doughty	Do you laugh, gentlewoman? [*To* MISTRESS GENEROUS] What say you to all these matters?
Mrs Generous	I will say nothing, but what you know, you know, And as the law shall find me let it take me.
Gillian	And so say I!
Mawd	And I!
Moll	And I! 200 Other confession you get none from us.
Arthur	[*To* MEG] What say you, granny?
Meg	Mamilion, ho! Mamilion, Mamilion!
Arthur	Who's that you call?
Meg	My friend, my sweetheart, my Mamilion.
Mrs Generous, *Moll, Gillian, & Mawd*	You are not mad?
Doughty	Ah, ha! That's her devil, her incubus, I warrant. Take her off from the rest; they'll hurt her. Come hither, poor old woman. [*aside*] I'll dandle a witch a little. – Thou wilt speak, and tell the truth, and

shalt have favour, doubt not. Say, art not thou a   210
witch?

[MISTRESS GENEROUS, MOLL, GILLIAN,
and MAWD] *storm*

Meg	'Tis folly to dissemble. Yea, sir, I am one.
Doughty	And that Mamilion which thou call'st upon Is thy familiar devil, is't not? Nay, prithee speak.
Meg	Yes, sir.
Doughty	That's a good woman. How long hast Had's acquaintance, ha?
Meg	A matter of six years, sir.
Doughty	A pretty matter. What, was he like a man?
Meg	Yes, when I pleas'd.
Doughty	And then he lay with thee, Did he not sometimes?
Meg	'Tis folly to dissemble: Twice a week he never fail'd me.
Doughty	Hmm, and how, 220 And how a little? Was he a good bedfellow?
Meg	'Tis folly to speak worse of him than he is.
Doughty	Ay, trust me is't. Give the devil his due.
Meg	He pleas'd me well, sir, like a proper man.
Doughty	There was sweet coupling?
Meg	Only his flesh felt cold.
Arthur	He wanted his great fires about him that

	He has at home.
Doughty	Peace! And did he wear good clothes?
Meg	Gentleman like, but black, black points and all.
Doughty	Ay, very like his points were black enough. But come, we'll trifle wi' ye no longer. Now shall you 230 all to the Justices, and let them take order with you till the 'sizes, and then let law take his course, and *Vivat Rex!* Master Generous, I am sorry for your cause of sorrow; we shall not have your company?
Generous	No, sir, my prayers for her soul's recovery Shall not be wanting to her, but mine eyes Must never see her more.
Robert	Moll, adieu sweet Moll! Ride your next journey with the company you have there. 240
Moll	Well, rogue, I may live to ride in a coach before I come to the gallows yet.
Robert	[*To* MISTRESS GENEROUS] And mistress, the horse that stays for you rides better with a halter than your jingling bridle. *Exit with* GENEROUS
Doughty	Master Seely, I rejoice for your family's atonement.
Seely	And I praise heaven for you that were the means to it.
Doughty	[*To the Constable and Officers*] On afore, drovers, with your untoward cattle. 250

Exit [Constable, Officers, MISTRESS
GENEROUS, MOLL, GILLIAN, MAWD, *and*
MEG] *severally*

Bantam	[*To* WHETSTONE] Why do not you follow, Master By-blow? I thank your aunt for the trick she would have fathered us withal.
Whetstone	Well, sir, mine aunt's mine aunt, and for that trick I will not leave her till I see her do a worse. *Exit*
Bantam	You're a kind kinsman!

Exeunt. Flourish

FINIS

[*Enter* EPILOGUE]

Now, while the witches must expect their due
By lawful justice, we appeal to you
For favourable censure. What their crime
May bring upon 'em, ripeness yet of time
Has not reveal'd. Perhaps great mercy may
After just condemnation give them day
Of longer life. We represent as much
As they have done before law's hand did touch
Upon their guilt, but dare not hold it fit
That we for justices and judges sit,   10
And personate their grave wisdoms on the stage
Whom we are bound to honour. No, the age
Allows it not. Therefore unto the laws
We can but bring the witches and their cause,
And there we leave 'em, as their devils did.
Should we go further with 'em? Wit forbid!
What of their story further shall ensue,
We must refer to Time, ourselves to you.   [*Exit*]

GLOSSARIAL NOTES

In these notes the label 'Barber' indicates that a gloss derives from Thomas Heywood and Richard Brome, *The Late Lancashire Witches* edited by Laird H. Barber (New York: Garland, 1979).

Dramatis Personae

3-4 *SHAKESTONE & BANTAM*   The names of Arthur's two friends indicate their youthful vigour. To 'shake' an animal is to worry it (OED shake *v.* 8c) and Shakestone's prey is Whetstone. Shakestone's name also suggests genital waving ('a testicle' OED stone *n.* 11a). A bantam is a small aggressive cock.

8 *ROBERT*   also called Robin, a diminutive or familiar version of the same name.

Prologue

1 *Corrantoes* early newspapers, prohibited 1632-38, hence 'failing'

1 *no foot-post late* no recent news

5 *ground the scene* set this play

agitation preparation for performance

7 *fat jailor* apparently a topical reference, now unknown

1.1

1-2 *Was ever crossed . . . in th' height?* Was ever exciting sport so deprived of its climax?

20 *matches* of equal acuity

21 *muse* a gap in a fence or hedge

23 *earth'd* hidden in a hole

39 *braver* more impressive

port manner of behaving

40 *state* financial prosperity

	unshaken steadfast
45	*wind* talk (to rhyme with 'sinned' not 'bind')
48	*mess* group
50	*coxcomb* fool (from the name of a professional fool's cap)
54	*out upon him* an expression of disgust
69	*lustick* merry
70	*froligozone* frolicsome
82-83	*I never heard . . . truth till now.* Although Whetstone's name evokes the punishment of liars (who had whetstones placed around their necks), and despite's Arthur's accusation here, Whetstone's character develops as a simpleton, not a liar. Possibly Heywood and Brome had not settled this.
87	*I think you are a witch* conventional response to someone who has guessed one's intentions
101	*beldams* mannish hags
108	*By-blow* a bastard ('one who comes into the world by a side-stroke OED by-blow *n.* 3), hence in claiming this as his father's family name Whetsone impugns his mother's virtue
109-12	*you came in at the window . . . like my grandam's cat, to leap over the hatch* stealthy methods of entry implying an illegitimate start in life (as the Bastard in Shakespeare's *King John* puts it, 'In at the window, or else o'er the hatch' 1.1.171)
134	*entire* affectionately attach
138	*surname* By-blow is Whetstone's *sire*-name from his father
139-41	*noverint universi per praesentes* the formulaic first words of a writ ('let all men know by these presents'), from which *noverint* had come to mean a scrivener
142	*As in praesenti* 'As in the present tense', the beginning of a well-known Latin verse used as a mnemonic for verse forms, and here with a possible pun on asinine
146	*Accidence* the first part of a Latin grammar book, dealing with inflections ('accidents') of word
	Mentiri nonest meum 'it is not for me to lie' (Latin)

149	*Ignaro* ignorant
153	*strain* characteristic way of behaving
224	*one slips no advantages* one who misses no opportunities for gain

[1.2]

59	*look off on't* look away from it
87	*at the ale* at the alehouse
87-88	*a fourpenny club* Seely's portion of a shared bill
91	*tester* a teston, worth sixpence
96	*double ringed tokens* privately issued tokens worth a farthing, hence Seely's loss was just two pence (Barber)
	rubbers best of three sets (or five, seven, etc.)
113-14	*what the foul evil* equivalent to 'what the devil?'
119	*weary o' the womb of him* tired of being inside him
124-25	*telling him his own* telling him some home truths
127	*carl* a base fellow, a churl
128-29	*He served you but well to baste ye for't* You deserve to be beaten for it
130-31	*but an I fall foul with ye, and I swaddle ye not savourly* but if you incur my displeasure and I do not beat you soundly
131	*brast* burst
136	*trow* suppose/think
146	*law in Lancashire* Lancashire kept its own legal system until the middle of the nineteenth century
149	*Daughter, I say –* Joan is interrupted by Winny, who then misinterprets these first three words as an answer.
153	*take such courses* behave in such a way
163	*the Scottish weird sisters* the three witches in Shakespeare's *Macbeth* (so named at 1.3.30, 2.1.19, 3.4.132, and 4.1.152)
164	*hiccup* 'A spasmodic affection of some other organ [than the diaphragm]' (OED hiccup *n.* b, citing this usage). Her allusion to Shakespeare's *Macbeth* seems to increase the intensity of the spell working upon Winny: her vision is disturbed and she explicitly swaps roles with her mother. The greening of Winny's vision might

be an allusion to green-sickness, an adolescent anaemia thought to
be caused by sexual longing, hence Joan's song on the theme of
unwanted pregnancy.

166   *white girl*   darling daughter (apparently invented here by analogy
with OED white boy 1)

170   *deft*   handsome

171   *langtidown dilly*   a meaningless refrain

179   *fadge*   proceed

187   *list*   like

189   *lessen*   unless

190   *with a wanion*   with a vengeance (OED wanion)

201-202   *You shall as soon . . . in the mouth with*   There's nothing you can do
to shut me up with

203   *shoen*   shoes

204   *sicky*   suchlike (OED sic-like)

206-207   *ween 'a'*   we would have

207   *Wot'st thou what?*   what do you know?

209   *the fond waxen wild, trow I*   the affectionate turned aggressive, I
suppose (referring to Lawrence's harsh words to her)

211-12   *our love shall be at an end*   our courtship must end (because we shall
marry), with unintentional comic suggest of loveless marriage

213   *mu'*   must (Q's 'mun' carries overtones of may)

214   *limmer loon*   mad rogue

215   *trow*   think

218   *sickerly*   with certainty
         jam   abuse

220   *flam*   mock

235   *i'fackins*   i' faith (a mild oath)

238   *bespeak*   arrange for

240   *'pparelments*   equipment and fittings (OED apparelment) and not
confined to apparel

241   *trickly*   Neatly, smartly

2.1

0 SD   *severally*   one by one but not necessarily from different directions

4 SP   *Meg*. Four witches are called for in the opening stage direction but only three are named in the scene (Meg, Mawd, and Gillian). The fourth (whom the audience would not have seen before in any case) may be Mistress Generous or Moll; possibly this matter was not settled in the manuscript. Q's repeated speech prefix for Meg is clearly wrong, and it is easier to imagine this as a compositorial misreading of 'Moll' than of 'Mrs Generous' or 'Goody Dickinson'.

11   It is possible that 'Mawd' was a speech prefix which the printer, mistaking its terminal period for a comma, misread as part of Gillian's line. Weighing against this interpretation, however, is the printed line's consistency with the iambic tetrameters that surround it.

13   *puggy*   an affectionate form of *pug* meaning a small demon (also spelt *puck*)

15   *meat*   nourishment, not confined to animal flesh

17   *a round*   'a dance in which the performers move in a circle or ring' (OED round n^1 11a)

18   *cockle*   a weed with black seeds which thrives in wheat fields (OED cockle n^1) or a similar looking disease of wheat caused by worms (OED cockle n^7), or possibly, by confusion, both

   darnel   another weed common in corn fields

   poppia   a dialect name for the cockle weed (OED poppy *n*. 2)

21   *our masque*   the dance the witches have just completed

54   *wat*   hare (OED wat^2)

63   *The devil on Dun*   the devil on horseback, from 'Dun', a quasi-proper name for any horse

69   *Peg*   a pet form of Margaret, as is Meg

   grizzled   grey coloured (the hare will have fur the colour of Meg's hair)

70   *gaunt thin gut*   as befits a greyhound

[2.2]

47   *bait* 'To set on dogs to bite and worry' (OED baite v² 2)

51   *relieve*   feed (Barber)

52   *course*   'a race of dogs (after a hare, etc.)' (OED course *n.* 7a)

54-59 *'Tis said hares . . . Pliny lies too*   In *Naturalis Historia* Book 8 Pliny attributes this idea to Archelaus (Barber)

56-57 *that which begets this year brings young ones the next*   the male begeter becomes female

66   *Robin*   a familiar form of his proper name, Robert

119   *tester*   a teston, worth sixpence

147   *Ipsitate*   Barber suggests 'perhaps a superlative of Latin *ipse* meaning "the very thing," "Mere quintessence of wine."' (as Generous called it at line 139)

154-55 *be with thee to bring*   be with you to achieve a determined result. Here the sense is sexual but other outcomes may be implied by 'to bring'.

166   *country*   native region (OED country 4), here Yorkshire (see line 179)

168   *in that name*   pretending to be a soldier

172   *Polack*   a native of Poland, used (like 'Russian') to mean the nation

178   *What countryman?*   Of where are you a countryman (native)?

196   Q's reading of grinding 'flesh' to powder is absurd, and the obvious intended opposition is 'flesh' and 'bones'.

198   *cat o' mountains*   a large feline animal such as leopard, panther, or tiger

199   *in red-and-white*   a variation on the figurative 'in black-and-white' (writing) also meaning 'attested by indisputable evidence', his bloodied flesh

214   *fitters*   fragments

238   *stand it all danger*   withstand it whatever the dangers

[2.3]

0 SD   *switch*   'a thin flexible shoot cut from a tree' (OED switch *n.* 2a)

1	*bullace* wild plums
3	*coursing* chasing hares with dogs
5.1 SD	*invisible* how this was indicated to the audience (costume?, demeanour?) is uncertain
	John Adson musician and composer (1587-1640), a specialist in wind instruments and masque music. Adson's 'new airs' are mentioned in 4.1 of Cavendish's *The Country Captain*, another King's men play.
5.1-2 SD	*a brace of greyhounds* Gillian and her Puckling in the guise of dogs, as promised at 2.1.56-7
8	*slips* quick-release leashes arranged to free two dogs at once when coursing (OED slip *n*³ 3a)

[2.4]

1	*piece* a gold sovereign coin, worth 11 shillings (OED piece *n* 13b). This sense Whetstone seems not to know (see lines 9-10) and is teased for it.
2	*pied* of more than one colour
11	*double rings* see note to 1.2.96
13	*take on* accept the bet
14	*cover these* match these coins with your own
24	*More than . . . fall of leaf* suggesting that Whetstone is losing hair, a sign of venereal disease. There follows a series of sexual puns on hare and pubic hair.
28	*birds' nests* women's pubic hair. The Nurse makes the same joke in Shakespeare's *Romeo and Juliet* 2.4.74.
32	*angle* fishing hook, and by extension the line and rod also
	angle...line...hare possibly sexual puns on female pubic delta (*angle*), penis (*line*), and pubic hair (*hare*)
47	*off the score* 'break out suddenly into impetuous speech or action' (OED score 3b)
50-52	*thine ears . . . lost them by scribbling* the punishment for seditious writing was the cropping of an ear, as happened to William Prynne

for his *Histriomastix* (1633)

53   *Bullfinch*   an attractive bird easily trained for singing (hence Whetstone will 'sing', complain, to his aunt and uncle)

56   *I am a bastard*   Like Shakespeare's Dogberry, Whetstone makes the comic error of repeating an insult ('I am an ass', *Much Ado About Nothing* 4.2.74 and 5.1.248)

58-59   *good old gentleman*   that is, Generous

59   *baffled*   disgraced

63   *law*   'An allowance in time or distance made to an animal that is to be hunted' (OED law n^1 20a)

[2.5]

1   *Halloo*   a cry to excite dogs

3   *lither*   'lazy, sluggish, spiritless' (OED lither *a.*)

4   *tykes*   low-bred, coarse, dogs

5   *with a wanion*   with a vengeance (OED wanion)

11-12   *not lash . . . switch will hold*   a moderate, not a thorough, lashing with merely a switch (see 2.3.0n). The first 'lash' might also carry the punning senses of 'rebuke' (OED lash $v.^1$ 6c) or 'comb' (OED lash $v.^3$).

15 SD   Gillian was the witch who said she would become a greyhound (2.1.56-57), and appears to be the character Q hereafter identifies as Goody Dickinson. Q's direction indicates the 'disappearing' part of the magical transformation (the dogs exit) but leaves no clue how the 'appearing' was managed.

19   *gammer*   'A rustic title for an old woman' (OED). The Boy says '*my* gammer' (a corruption of 'grandmother') because small communities use kin terms even where no biological connection is implied.

42·   *la*   'An exclamation formerly used to introduce or accompany a conventional phrase or an address, or to call attention to an emphatic statement' (OED la *int.*). In Shakespeare *The Merry Wives of Windsor* Slender uses a similar construction: 'You do yourself wrong, indeed, la' (1.1.292-3).

50 SD   The simplest staging of the transformation of the demon-child into a white horse is a mere report of it happening off stage.

[2.6]

7   Cut 'A familiar expression for a common or labouring horse' (OED cut n^2 29)

10   *curry-comb time*] the early morning rubbing down (currying) of a horse with a comb

15-16   *the divinity of the Mitre*   the fine wine of The Mitre tavern in London

18   *a puritan . . . the Mitre*   the tavern's name comes from the headgear of a bishop, reviled by puritans for its sumptuousness

19   *Robert*   Moll uses the proper name to sound formal and reproving

21-22   *an be ruled*   if you'll be ruled

27   *because*   so that

34   *fit*   punish (OED fit v^1 12)

48   *Light*   like *'Slight*, an abbreviation of *God's light*, a mild oath

49   *all the milk shall*   all the milk which shall

51   *the proverb of the bishop's foot*   a pot of burnt food was said to have had the bishop's foot in it (Barber)

59   *trussed*   'Knit together, compactly framed or formed' (OED trussed *ppla*. 1b)

65   *look your horse*   look for your horse

67   *Stand up!*   a cry to urge on a horse (OED stand *v*. 103h)

3.1

2   *break the cake over the bride's head*   a Northern wedding tradition (Barber)

5   *lost the church*   missed the church ceremony

9   *frolic*   frolicsome
     crank   high-spirited

19   *brag*   cheerful

	carries it promotes it
25	*ring backwards* from bass to treble, usually reserved for an emergency warning (Barber)
26	*I'fack* I'faith, a mild oath
28	*merry conceit of the stretch-ropes* Seely interprets the emergency signal as the bell-ringers' joke about the enormous fire in his kitchen (which is cooking the feast)
36	*fare* be entertained with food (OED fare v¹ 8)
37	*cate* delicacy
40	*'Slid* abbreviation of *God's lid*, a mild oath
45 SD	*the battle* apparently a musical style used to represent or accompany fighting. That the instruments need not be noisy is indicated by the opening direction of Marston's *Antonio and Mellida* 'The cornets sound a battle within'
46 SD	The spirit cannot be seen by the guests, hence their amazement
55-56	*woe worth it* a curse on it (OED woe int. 4a)
60	*Pax* Latin for *peace*, hence 'be quiet'
61	*law-day* day of meeting of court of law, used by vaguely-aggrieved Gregory to mean 'day for settling scores'
64	*warrant* protect
74	*country* native region, here Lancashire
82	*The dresser calls in* A servant signals that the food is ready by knocking upon the table (the 'dresser') from which it is served. *fare* be entertained with food (OED fare v¹ 8)
86	*messes* groups of persons sitting together and served from the same dishes. Here each mess is ten persons, hence the large quantities.
92	*Florentines* a kind of pie or tart, possibly of meat
98	*doubler* a large plate or dish
107	*'Zooks* short for gadzooks, a mild oath
124	*humble-bees* bumble-bees (an alternative name)
125	*Jew's-ears* An edible fungus growing on the roots and trunks of trees
126	*puckfists* puff-balls, a fungus with ball-shaped spore cases

cow-shards cow-pats (solidified puddles of dung)

139 *borne* carried (that is, out of the house because drunk)

165 *cheer* provisions (OED cheer *n*1 6a)

deceptio visus deceptive spectacle

165-66 *the former store has 'scaped 'em* the food set aside earlier is unaffected

167 *good 'em* do good to them

[3.2]

9 *forgi'* forgive

11-12 *to his . . . in a day* apparently a topical allusion, now lost

22 *'a'* ha' (meaning, 'have')

29 *that you might* so that you might

58 *considered* paid (OED consider *v.* 8)

64 *acquittance* receipt for the repayment of a debt

67-69 *lose it . . . find it . . . conceal it* an archaic form of the subjunctive mood equivalent to 'have lost it . . . have found it . . . concealed it'

73-74 *nettled . . . nettled* irritated . . . aroused (OED nettle *v.* 2 and 3)

75 *raw-boned* having projecting bones

78 *rank riding* reckless fast riding of a horse (OED rank *a.* 3b), with connotation of sexual 'riding' via 'ramp rider' (OED ramp *a.*) and 'lustful, licentious; in heat' (OED rank *a.* 13)

82 *'Sfoot* shortened form of *God's foot*, a mild oath

94 *case* physical condition (OED case n^1 5b)

[3.3]

27 *husbandman* farmer

39 *baffle* disgrace

57 *'Zooks* short for gadzooks, a mild oath

60 *a fly touched it* if Moll's intention was to trivialize what he saw, the association of flies with the devil ironically heightens Doughty's suspicion

62 *blast* blight (OED blast *v.* 8a)

64 SD *Sellenger's Round* music to a popular country dance, also known as

'The Beginning of the World'. The music is reproduced in William Chappell, *Popular Music of the Olden Time* (New York: Dover, 1965) 1:69-71.

67   *family of love*   alluding to a reactionary Dutch religious sect of that name, popular in England, which advocated absolute obedience to established authorities

78   *spin two-penny tow*   the kind of processing of flax which might be done in a workhouse, hence a strong threat (Barber)

96   *sorrel sops*   pieces of bread soaked in a sauce made from sorrel, a sour herb

100   *stomach*   lustful desire (OED stomach *n.* 1g, 5b)

102   *a-good*   heartily

108   *'The Beginning of the World'*   another name for 'Sellenger's Round'; see 3.3.64 SDn above.

114   *'The Running o' the Country'*   'presumably one of the old dance tunes' (Barber)

123   *point*   a lace for the tying together parts of clothing (such as a doublet and breeches) where buttons would now be used (OED point *n*[1] B5). Like a button, a point could stand for something of little value, hence Lawrence and Doughty think Moll is making a joke, lines 126 and 133.

135   *when all your points are ta'en away*   'At the end of a wedding day the bridegroom's friends undressed him and took away his points by way of preparing him for the bride' (Barber)

136   *slops*   wide loose trousers (OED slop *n*[1] 4)

142   *I's never be jealous the more for that*   I shall never be more jealous for that reason

157   *scuffling for the Tutbury bull*   alluding to a minstrels' sport in Tutbury on the Staffordshire/Derbyshire border in which one team tried to drive a bull across the river Dove and the other team tried to prevent it (Barber)

170   *hornpipe*   a vigorous dance to the accompaniment of a wind instrument

posset   a hot drink of milk, liquor and spice, often drunk before retiring

187   *trim*   elegantly dressed

192   *what's here to do?*   what's the matter here? (OED do *v*. 33)

4.1

15-17   *how damnably . . . rid now*   last night's 'riding' was with Moll, and now the sexual connotation is less pleasing to Robert

19   *Gramercy*   thanks

21   *Aesop's ass*   allusion to the story of an ass who, although carrying food, eat whatever grew along his way

24   *Cut*   'A familiar expression for a common or labouring horse' (OED cut n^2 29)

26   *tail*   vagina

28   *cheer*   provisions (OED cheer *n*1 6a)

35-36   *'Horse, horse . . . carry me'*   the spell Mistress Generous used when first bridling him at 3.2.103-104

42-43   *deep ditch . . quick-set*   the edge of the stage treated as a ditch, and the standing audience as a hedge made from plant cuttings (OED quickset *n*.1)

48   *beldams*   mannish hags

      cramming   eating greedily (OED cram *v*. 2b)

53   *demur*   delay (between courses)

57   *As chief*   most important of all (chiefly)

65   *sod*   boiled (OED sod *ppla.*)

73   *leese*   lose

78   *nab*   not in OED; apparently a familiar spirit (Barber)

82   *Nan*   grandmother, a familiar form of address of an older women by an unrelated younger women. Both women have 'ridden' Robert.

91-93   *if they . . . presently*   if they are about to have liquid food (spoon-meat) they probably are nearly finished their feast

95   *cheer*   provisions (OED cheer *n*1 6a)

107-24   In Q this song is printed at the end of the play (on L4r) under the
          label 'Song. II. Act.', although this location in Act Four seems to
          need it more. Lines have been assigned to particular witches
          according to the names of the familiar spirits where mentioned.

111   *huggy*   hug ye

120   *store*   provide for

126   *shift for myself*   look out for my own interests (OED shift *v.* 7a)

138 SP   *Where's my Mamilion*   assigned to '2.' in Q, but Meg called her
          familiar this name at 2.1.13

139 SP   *And my incubus*   assigned to '1.' in Q
          My tiger to be bestrid   assigned to '3.' in Q

145   *try conclusions*   see which of us is the stronger (OED conclusion *n.*
          8b)

                                    [4.2]

15   *sunder beds*   sleep separately

28   *plight*   condition (OED plight *n.*^{2} 5)

30   *bate an ace*   lose a jot (OED ace *n.* 3b)

33   *late*   lately

46   *gramercy*   thanks

49-50   *tied to . . . confess something*   Robert, having overpowered her since
          the end of 4.1, has bridled Mistress Generous (which turned her
          into a horse) and tied her in the stables. Here he likens her state to
          one tied to the rack of torture, as witches might be.

53   *spurred*   pricked by spurs

55   *sore travailed*   worked hard

76   *currying*   the grooming of a horse with a comb

79   *caparisons*   ornamented cloths worn by a horse

114   *believe no witches*   believe there are no witches

127   Although Q's reading *juggling* (meaning 'that which is part of a
          deception') would be an appropriate adjective here, Mrs Generous
          makes clear that the bridle jingles at 4.1.1.

130   *engine*   device, with strong connotations of 'snare' (OED engine *n.*

	3 and 5c)
134	If not a misprint, Q's reading 'of' is an archaism (OED *of prep.* 55a)
142	*meander* bewilderingly complicated situation (OED meander *n.* 2c)
143	*intricated* entangled
148	*chary* careful
156	*Lift up . . . yon hills* 'a reference to Psalm 121:1 "I will lift up mine eyes unto the hills, from whence cometh my help"' (Barber)
158	*horrid dwelling* whatever earthly benefit she got by her dealing with the devil
167	*promis'd to the stake* burning at the stake was a continental punishment for witchcraft, while in England hanging was used. Generous is not quite making sense, since the punishment follows discovery of the compact and cannot be a substitute for it
173	*how far doth that contract stretch?* what have you signed away?
175	*his part that made it* God's part
183	*penitent tears have power to quench* the power of sincere repentance was denied by extreme Protestantism. Lancashire, however, was still a centre of Catholic dissent
191	*presume't* take upon myself the authority to forgive her
199	*as I do . . . pardon me* as I pardon you, so heaven pardon me for presuming to do this (see line 191)
204	*passed* mutually interchanged (OED pass *v.* 9)
215	*Too little all* our combined tears are insufficient
221	*My wife, sister, and daughter* as all things to me
227	*journey-man* means of travel, with a pun on journeyman meaning a qualified tradesman working for daily pay (as opposed to being a master)

[4.3]

5	*bouncing* bragging (OED bouncing *vbl. n.* 3, with this example)
24	*disposers* managers of their own affairs
26	*to thrust them out on't* to throw them (the Seelys) out of the house

30-31   *some wholesome . . . the commonwealth*   legal proceedings to take protective control of the Seelys' property during their temporary insanity

35   *as far to seek of*   no nearer knowing

40   *lay*   search (OED lay *v.*[1] 18c)

41-43   *the purpose . . . lease be out*   '. . . in some cases, the devil set a definite time when he would come and fetch the witch who had dedicated herself to him' (Barber)

44   *skimmington*   a parodic procession led by impersonators or mannequins of a married couple intended to mock their domestic strife

51   *Ware wedlock, ho!*   look out, here comes wedlock! (OED ware *v.* 3). Shakespeare's Thersites uses the same construction: 'The bull has the game. Ware horns, ho!' (*Troilus and Cressida* 5.8.3-4)

62   *want of bedstaves?*   because broken by the couple's vigorous lovemaking, a typical crudity concerning newlyweds

63   *better implement*   an erect penis to consummate the marriage

64   *a homely tale*   plain truth

66   *greedy worm*   passionate desire (OED worm *n.* 11c)

68   *mickle*   great

76   *ligatory*   binding. 'Impotence was often blamed on witches, and "ligation" (binding) was the technical term for this activity' (Barber

82   *undertake*   deal with (with connotation of 'have sex with')

86   *hoydens*   ill-mannered, low-class boors

92   *wot*   knows

93   *trow*   think

93-94   *Gaffer Do-Nought*   Mister Do-Nothing. Gaffer was usually a title respectful of age and/or seniority

94   *woe worth*   a curse on (OED woe *int.* 4a)

100   *swag-bellied*   paunchy

102 SP   The answer to this question is provided in language that suits Doughty, so (contrary to Q's reading) the questioner should be someone else. Lawrence perhaps stands apart from the trio Arthur,

Bantam, and Shakestone comforting Parnell.

113   *cozened*   deceived
122   *jury of women*   such juries examine the bodies of women claiming non-consummation of marriage and women accused of witchcraft (See Diane Purkiss *The Witch in History,* London 1996, pp. 231-49)
125-26 *in this case*   under these circumstances, but also punning on 'case' as vagina. Although unrecorded by OED, Shakespeare commonly used this slang, eg Mistress Quickly's 'Vengeance of Jenny's case! Fir on her!' *Merry Wives of Windsor* 4.1.56
127   *out of a doing case*   unfit for sexual 'doing'
133   *mind*   intention (OED mind $n.^{1}$ 10)
145   *maleficium versus hanc*   'A curse upon . . .', the legal term for magic causing impotence
148   *lere*   knowledge
153   *now right*   right now
156   *casten*   cast
        an't   if not
158   *bean-cod*   bean-pod
164   *con*   understand
165   *stay*   remain during
167   *ware*   teach them to beware (OED ware $v.^{1}$ 5, with this example)
        mell or ma'   meddle (OED mell $v.^{2}$ 8b)
168   *testril*   a teston, worth sixpence
        longie   'a lout . . . see the OED entry under "lungis" whose variant "longis" is suggested here as the basis of Parnell's word *longie*' (Barber)
169   *losel*   good-for-nothing
170   *ma'*   may or make, either fits the sense
        warplin   'new-born thing . . . ie Lawrence impotent as a baby' (Barber)
171   *boggle*   fumble with
172   *trow*   think
173.1-2 SD *skimmington and his wife*   these appear to be mannequins; see

	note to line 44 above
173.2 SD	*country rustics* peasants
173.6 SD	*alarm* a sound make to call men to arms
173.7 SD	*hoydens* ill-mannered, low-class boors
173.8 SD	*vail bonnet* take of their head-wear to show submission and deference (OED bonnet *n.* 1a)
180	*this* the beating
	gang walk
185	*you . . . ticklers!* alluding again to Lawrence's impotence: he can only tickle a woman
187	*ladle* the OED etymology suggests that *skimmington* might derive from a wife's beating of her husband with her skimming ladle

[4.4]

12	*halt* hobble
	downright entirely
21	*rack and manger* 'a play on the phrase "to lie at rack and manger" which meant "to live in luxury"' (Barber)
33	*Naunt* my aunt (shortened from 'mine aunt')
43	*table* table guests

[4.5]

3	*chamber* chamber-pot, or more precisely the urine in it
4	*short banquet* dessert of sweets and fruit (OED banquet *n.*[1] 3)
18	*fain* gladly
29	*all one* originally 'not a matter of choice', but here in the derived sense of 'does not matter' (OED all C *adv.* 5)
32.1 SD	*pedant* child's tutor
32.2 SD	*strain* melody (OED strain *n.*[2] 13)
36	*In his . . . your father* In the house of him (your mother's husband) who is thought to be your father. The pedant was 'in his house' in several senses: taking his place, intruding into his bloodline (the house of Bantam), and, possibly, occupying his wife's vagina (OED

house *n.*[1] 7c)

38	*Nise prius* Latin for 'Unless previously', the first words of a writ served on a sheriff to further a legal case at the county assizes.
39	*'sizes* assizes, county courts of civil and criminal justice
41	*tail* bottom
48	*otherwise* other way
66.1 SD	*switch* 'a thin flexible shoot cut from a tree' (OED switch *n.* 2a)
	curry-comb instrument for rubbing down a horse
72	*Lord President's court in York* The king's deputy ruling the six northern counties (Barber)
72-73	*stood for his attorney* took his place as though his agent
74	*amort* still, as though dead
86	*By-blows* bastards
89	*health* a drink in honour of good health (OED health *n.* 6)
90	*fain* gladly
101	*pug* puck, a small demon

5.1

1	*country* native region (OED country 4), here Lancashire
4	*'Zooks* short for gadzooks, a mild oath
10	*dogged* having the bad qualities of a dog
12	*worry* seize by the throat
17	*stout* brave and resolute
35-36	*could not make a bit of butter* witches were commonly blamed when cream could not be churned into butter. Shakespeare's Robin Goodfellow (a puck) is said to 'bootless make the breathless housewife churn' (*A Midsummer Night's Dream*, 2.1.37)
41	*gear* foul stuff (OED gear *n.* 10)
45	*wry* twisted
52	*for me* on my behalf
58	*After you* Doughty accepts being a kind of second father to the boy
	Gossip godparent
61	*dog-tricks* treacherous, spiteful acts

	horse-tricks using people and animals like horses
86	*but by* except that he is distinguishable by
87	*horse-corser* dealer in horses. Like modern used-car sellers, these were proverbial deceitful.
99	*folks* relatives
100	*Gritty* millers were often suspected of adulterating flour with cheap materials, which would make the end products taste gritty
	close secret (OED close adj. A7)
103	*cuff-devil* devil thumper

[5.2]

10	*Morglay* name of the sword owned by mythical hero Sir Bevis of Hampton
	comrogue fellow rogue
13	*Gib* familiar name for a male cat
	Askapart name of the giant killed by Sir Bevis (see note to line 10
15	*brave* fine, describing the lodging, not the soldier
17.3 SD	*several* separate, not necessarily more than two
22	*Laplands* Lapland was the fabled home of witches
23.2 SD	*starts* leaps up suddenly
30	*have at you* cry to accompany a strike (as with 'take that!')
32	*light on* landed a blow on (OED light v.¹ 10a)

[5.3]

27	*mere* complete and unaided (OED mere adj. A 2, 4)
40	*blaz'd* proclaimed (OED blaze v.² 2)
49	*sunder'd* parted
66	*fain* gladly
71	*murrain* pestilence
78	*bilbo* a high quality sword, named after Bilbao, Spain, where they were made
83	*Fast or loose* an old confidence trick game in which a seemingly knotted cord is freed from a stick. The Soldier claims a small

success against the equally 'slippery' spirits.

90   *scot-free*   without paying a 'reckoning' (scot)

92   *tract*   trace (OED tract *n.*³ 11)

100   *last age*   period before the end of time, which Christian mythology predicted would be a time of miracles (benign and evil)

103   *my great incredulity*   refusal to believe in witchcraft

106   *Know you . . . read it*   hand could also mean handwriting, and since the amputated hand informs Generous about its owner, he takes the enquiry thus.

112-13 *tenants at will*   tenants without security of tenure, liable to be evicted anytime at the owner's will

113   rent-free   without paying rent, but also possibly punning on 'rent' meaning 'gash' or 'cut'

115   *hand*   as in line 106, this puns on the meaning 'handwriting'

[5.4]

14   *sic is 'so'*   As in 1.1, Whetstone shows basic Latin knowledge

24   *stay*   support (OED stay *n.*²) , with pun on 'place of sojourn' (OED stay *n.*³ 6b)

32   *qualm*   sickness

40   *shrewd*   severe

45   *their beating*   '. . . pulse was formerly sometimes misconstrued as a plural' (Barber)

49   *prove*   test (OED prove *v.* 1a)

55   *testate*   witness (OED testate *n.* B1)

57   *handy-dandy*   children's game of guessing which of two closed fists contains a small object

70   *inundant*   overflowing

[5.5]

1   *country*   native region (OED country 4), here Lancashire

2   *Lapland*   the fabled home of witches (as at 5.2.22)

9   *taken a course*   instigated a pursuit (OED course *n.* 7a)

17	*quean*	whore

17   *quean*   whore
18 SD   This and Shakestone's ensuing comment indicate that, no longer bewitched, the servants are again appropriately dressed. Q's 'first habits' is misleading since at their first entrance Lawrence and Parnell were already bewitched.
40-41   Q's reading of 'witched worch' might mean 'bewitched pain' (OED wark *n.*¹), but the context seems to demand something more simple
41   *woe worth*   a curse on (OED woe *int.* 4a)
42   *made all so nought*   made everything (his penis) so useless
45   *to do*   what to do
59   *only*   only until
63   *swink*   toil
65   *painful*   painstaking (OED painful *a.* 5)
67   *hea'en*   heaven
67-68   *are a-was*   have become (Barber)
69   *anenst*   among/against (OED anent *prep.* 8)
78   *instructive*   (a son) apt to be instructed
91   *untoward*   unruly
110   *bravest*   finest (OED brave *a.* 3)
119   *their witch*   the one that bewitched them
127-28   *saving his land . . . your distraction*   Seely was too busy with his own problems to help Arthur about this mortgage, as described at 1.1.242-69
137   *make sides*   divide yourselves into two parties: the witches and their enemies
147   *'sizes*   assizes, county courts of civil and criminal justice
149   *Naunt*   my aunt (shortened from 'mine aunt')
150   *'od's fish*   God's fish, a rare oath
158   *fardel*   pack
165   *bugs-words*   frightening speeches
166   *for*   from (OED for *prep.* 23d)
171-72   *wiser in commission for the peace*   the Justices of the Peace (inferior magistrates) who are 'in commission' in the sense of appointed for

the purpose

182   *switch*   'a thin flexible shoot cut from a tree' (OED *switch n.* 2a),
         which could be used as a horsewhip

198   *what you know, you know*   Shakespeare's Iago says the same thing in
         almost identical circumstances (*Othello* 5.2.309)

205   *You are not mad?*   Are you mad? (for confessing)

208   *dandle*   play with like a baby

211.2 SD   *storm*   struggle violently against their restraint

216   *Had's*   Had his

229   *like*   likely (OED *like* adj. 8)

232   *'sizes*   assizes, county courts of civil and criminal justice

232   *Vivat Rex!*   long live the king!

246   *atonement*   mutual reconciliation (OED *atonement n.* 1, 2)

249   *on afore*   go ahead
         drovers   drivers of cattle to market

250   *untoward*   unruly

250.3 SD *severally*   one by one but not necessarily from different directions

SYNOPSIS

The action of the play takes places in Lancashire, mostly at the homes of two squires, Seely and Generous. The first scene has three young 'blades', Arthur, Bantam, and Shakestone, debating the mysterious, perhaps supernatural, disappearance of a hare they were hunting. They are joined by Whetstone, a fool whom 'all the brave blades of the country use to whet their wits upon'. The young men are heading to sample the renowned hospitality of Master Generous, Whetstone's uncle, who has agreed to save Arthur from losing his lands to a usurious mortgagor. Ordinarily Arthur's uncle, Seely, might be expected to help, but Seely's household is in turmoil because all respect and deference has broken down. Seely's son Gregory and daughter Winny insult and bully their parents, and are in turn insulted and bullied by their respective servants Lawrence and Parnell. Thus newly raised in status, Lawrence and Parnell are able to marry at their former masters' expense, and the first act ends with the planning of celebrations for this event.

The second act begins with the villains of the piece, four witches, exulting at their success in bewitching the Seelys and planning further mischief. By changing themselves into greyhounds and leading the other dogs astray they plan to ruin the young men's hare-hunting. Generous bids farewell to his young guests, risen early for another day's recreation, and finds that his wife too has left the house on horseback. After instructing this groom Robert to deny her the horse next time, and to fetch wine from Lancaster, Generous is visited by a soldier who begs to be given work. His timing is perfect, for the man Generous has hired to run his mill resigns complaining of attacks at night by fierce cats. The soldier gladly takes the miller's place.

A truant schoolboy, bored of gorging on fruit, finds two greyhounds and leads them off in hope of a reward from their owner, while Bantam and Shakestone mock Whetstone's irritating stupidity despite their promise to tolerate him for the sake of Arthur's new relationship with Whetstone's uncle, Generous. The boy re-enters with the two greyhounds and begins to beat them for failing to chase a hare, when the dogs are suddenly transformed into a witch and her demon-child. The boy is bridled and kidnapped, to be taken to the witches' feast.

On his way to Lancaster, Generous's groom Robert stops off at the home of his sweetheart Moll, who offers to fly him to London and back overnight to fetch the wine his master prefers. Having seen her make her broom and pail move unaided, Robert agrees.

Act three begins with Seely and his wife Joan preparing the feast on the day of Lawrence and Parnell's marriage, which descends into farce as an unseen spirit transforms the food into stones, cowpats, and live animals. Unexpectedly Gregory and Winny are restored to their former obedience to their parents, so the remaining guests decide to stay and enjoy what food is left. At the Generous home, Robert has returned from London with the wine his master wanted, and proof that he has made the 300 mile journey overnight. Puzzled, Generous exits and Robert worries he will be punished for revealing what must be witchcraft. Mistress Generous asks Robert for her horse and, as instructed, Robert denies her. Infuriated, she bridles him and leads him off like a horse. Back at the wedding feast all seems well, although Seely and Joan fall out while their children display proper obedience. The spell on the Seely household has changed, not ended, and the musicians at the wedding find their instruments will yield no sound. Even sceptical Doughty concludes that witches are at work.

The reason the food disappeared from the wedding feast is apparent at the start of act four: it was needed for a secret witch-feast at a barn. One witch arrives there by badger, another arrives by bear, and Mistress Generous arrives on back of the groom Robert, who is tied up outside but peeps in to see the witches cavort with their familiar spirits. Spotting his chance, the boy the witches kidnapped escapes and the witches break up their celebrations to pursue him. Generous's suspicions are by now highly aroused, and on her return home Mistress Generous is forced to admit her pact with the devil, for which he forgives her upon a solemn promise to reform. With chaos still reigning in the Seely household, Doughty takes in the parents while Arthur takes in the children. Their servants are no better off. Parnell wants to annul the marriage because formerly lusty Lawrence is impotent since tying his codpiece with a charm given him by Moll, and the villagers are quick to perform a ritual mockery of the unhappy couple. Still galled by the insults of the young blades, Whetstone is assisted by his aunt, Mistress Generous, in achieving revenge by showing them their 'true' fathers, in each case a family servant.

At the mill the soldier is kept from sleeping by cat-like spirits, one of whom, Mistress Generous, loses a hand to the soldier's trusty Spanish sword. Thus forced to take to her bed, Mistress Generous cannot conceal her stump from her husband, who also has the cut-off member recovered from the mill. It is obvious that her repentance and reformation were feigned. Once convinced that witchcraft is about, Doughty acts quickly to capture the women responsible, at which point their charms fail. Lawrence is restored to vigour, he and Parnell to amity, and Mistress Generous is given over to the constable leading the other witches to the Lancaster assizes. In a final desperate effort the witches call unavailingly on their familiar spirits, and one breaks down and confesses her crime. Whetstone decides to stay with his aunt despite her crimes and is disinherited by Generous in favour of Arthur. The play ends with the witches led away to the indeterminate fate that was, at the time the play was first performed, the sensational news of London.

TEXTUAL NOTES

The play was first printed in a quarto of 1634 and the control text for the present edition is one of the two British Library copies of this quarto (shelfmark C.34.c.54). In keeping with *Globe Quartos* editorial criteria, no attempt was made to collate variation between early copies. James Orchard Halliwell-Phillipps published an edition of the play in 1853 and R. H. Shepherd included it in his dramatic works of Heywood in 1874, but neither provided notes or a modernized text. Laird H. Barber's edition of 1979 (New York, Garland) provided a facsimile and a transcription of the 1634 quarto with extensive notes, but the present edition is the first in modern spelling.

 The necessary modernization of the barely-comprehensible dialect of Parnell and Lawrence has greatly reduced their regional distinctiveness. The effort to retain something of their difference, and the treatment of terminal *n* in their speeches require special comment. Their dialect puts an *n* sound at the end of verbs, so that *must* or *may* becomes *mun*, *shall* becomes *shan*, and *have* becomes *han*. In this edition these have been elided to *ma'*, *sha'*, and *ha'*. Other verbs they end with *-en* on the Old English model, so *casten* is their past tense of *cast*. Where misunderstanding is likely these have been modernized. Thus *shoulden* and *woulden* have been changed to *should* and *would* to avoid confusion with *shouldn't* and *wouldn't*.

 The following abbreviations are used in the collation:

Halliwell-Phillipps	a reading from James Orchard Halliwell-Phillipps's 1853 edition
Shepherd	a reading from R. H. Shepherd's 1874 edition
(Barber)	a suggestion made in Laird H. Barber's 1979 edition
this edn	a reading originating in this edition

1.1

226	think] *Halliwell-Phillipps;* rhinke Q
253	been] *Shepherd;* hin Q
271	you] *Halliwell-Phillipps;* yon Q

[1.2]

5	conjure] *Shepherd;* conure Q
26	transgress] *Shepherd;* trangress Q
152	warrants] *Halliwell-Phillipps;* warrant Q
215	brains] *Halliwell-Phillipps;* braincs Q

2.1

4 SP	*Moll*] *this edn; Meg.* Q
12 SP	*Mawd*] *this edn;* not in Q

[2.2]

31	like] *Shepherd;* likes Q
37 SP	*Arthur*] *Halliwell-Phillipps; Gener.* Q.
196	bones] *Halliwell-Phillipps;* flesh Q

[2.3]

5.1 SD	*John*] *this edn; J.* Q
19 SD	*Exeunt*] *this edn; Exit.* Q

[2.4]

63 SD	*Exeunt*] *this edn; Exit.* Q

[2.5]

15.1 SD	GILLIAN] *this edn; Gooddy* Q.
15.2-3 SD	*a small . . . greyhounds*] *this edn; the Boy upon the dogs, going in.* Q
50	*what's*] *this edn; wher's* Q

3.1

34 SD   *Enter . . . WHETSTONE]* this edn; *Enter Musitians, Lawrence, Parnell, Win. Mal. Spencer, two Country Lasses, Doughty, Greg. Arthur, Shakton, Bantam, and Whetstone.* Q

46 SD   *Enter a spirit above*] this edn; *The Spirit appeares.* Q

81 SD   *Knocking . . . dresser*] this edn; *Knock within, as at dresser.* Q

93 SD   *Enter fiddlers . . . they enter*] this edn; *Enter Musitians playing before, Lawrence, Doughty, Arthur, Shakton, Bantam, Whetstone, and Gregory, with dishes*: *A Spirit (over the doore) does some action to the dishes as they enter.* Q

[3.3]

34   in] *Shepherd;* is Q

103 SD   *Fiddlers . . . tune*] this edn; *Musicke. Selengers round. As they beginne to daunce, they play another tune, then fall into many.* Q

108 SD   *The . . . tune*] this edn; *Musicke. Every one a severall tune.* Q

4.1

106 SD   *Each . . . song*] this edn; *Dance and Song together. In the time of which the Boy speaks.* Q

141 SD   ROBERT *. . . spirit*] this edn; *Robin stands amaz'd at this* Q

[4.2]

99   all my] *this edn;* my all Q

127   jingling] *this edn;* jugling Q

134   on] *this edn;* of Q

199   me] Q; thee *(Barber)*

[4.3]

102 SP   Lawrence] *this edn;* Dou. Q

[4.5]

43 SP	*Arthur, Shakestone, and Whetstone] this edn; All.* Q
52 SD	*Enter . . . face.] this edn; Enter a nimble Taylor dauncing, using the same posture to Shakstone.* Q
62 SP	*Arthur and Whetstone] this edn; All* Q
66 SD	*Enter . . . face.] this edn; Enter Robin with a switch and a Currycomb, he points at Arthur.* Q
78 SD	*Enter . . . face.] this edn; Enter a Gallant, as before to him.* Q
82 SP	*Arthur] this edn; Whet.* Q

5.1

52 SP	*Miller] Halliwell-Phillipps;* not in Q
58	*you] Shepherd;* yon Q

[5.2]

17 SD	*Enter . . . doors] this edn; Enter* Mrs. Generous, Mall, *all the Witches and their spirits (at severall dores.)* Q
23 SD	*The . . . starts] this edn; The Witches retire: the Spirits come about him with a dreadfull noise: he starts.* Q
30 SD	*He . . . bloodied] this edn; Beates them off, followes them in, and Enters againe.* Q

[5.3]

92 SD	*They . . . hand] this edn; Lookes about and findes the hand.* Q

[5.5]

18 SD	*proper] this edn; first* Q
40-41	*wicked witch] this edn; witched worch* Q
148	*Enter* GILLIAN, MAWD, MEG, *Constable, and Officers] this edn; Enter Witches, Constable, and Officers.* Q
211 SD	MISTRESS GENEROUS, MOLL, GILLIAN, *and* MAWD *storm] this edn; They storme.* Q

250 SD   *Exit Constable, Officers*, MISTRESS GENEROUS,
MOLL, GILLIAN, MAWD, and MEG *severally*]
this edn; Exeunt severally Q

The following is an extract from a letter from Nathaniel Tomkyns to Sir Robert Phelips of 16 August 1634. It was published by Herbert Berry in *Shakespeare's Playhouses* (New York: AMS Press, 1987) pp. 123-4, and is presented here in modernized spelling.

Here hath been lately a new comedy at the Globe called *The Witches of Lancashire*, acted by reason of the great concourse of people three days together. The third day I went with a friend to see it, and found a greater appearance of fine folk, gentlemen and gentlewomen, than I thought had been in town in the vacation. The subject was of the slights and passages done or supposed to be done by these witches sent from thence hither, and other witches and other witches and their familiars. Of their nightly meetings in several places, their banqueting with all sorts of meat and drink conveyed unto them by their familiars upon the pulling of a cord, the walking of pails of milk by themselves and (as they say of children) alone, the transforming of men and women into the shapes of several creatures and especially of horses by putting an enchanted bridle into their mouths, their posting to and from places far distant in an incredible short time, the cutting off a witch (= gentlewoman's) hand in the form of a cat by a soldier turned miller, known to her husband by a ring thereon (the only tragical part of the story), the representing of wrong and putative fathers in the shape of mean persons to gentlemen by way of derision, the tying of a knot at a marriage (after the French manner) to cease masculine ability, and the conveying away of the good cheer and bringing in a mock feast of bones and stones instead thereof and the filling of pies with living birds and young cats etcetera. And though there be not in it, to my understanding, any poetical genius, or art, or language, or judgement to state or tenet of witches (which I expected) or application to virtue, but full of ribaldry and of things improbable and impossible, yet in respect of the newness and the subject (the witches being still visible and in prison here) and in regard it consisteth from the beginning to the end of odd passages and fopperies to provoke laughter, and is mixed with diverse songs and dances, it passeth for a merry and excellent new play.

APPENDIX 2

The dramatists appear to have had access to witness statements taken in connection with the case of the Pendle witches. The most illuminating statement is that of Edmund Robinson which was published in John Webster, *The Displaying of Supposed Witchcraft* (London, 1677). This material is clearly the source for 2.3, 2.5, 4.1, and 5.1 and the miller's boy in the play corresponds to the real Edmund Robinson. In the following extract from Webster's book (sigs. Yy2r-Yy3r) the spelling and dating have been modernized.

The examination of Edmund Robinson, son of Edmund Robinson of Pendle Forest, eleven years of age, taken at Padham before Richard Shuttleworth and John Starkey Esquires, two of his majesty's justices of the peace within the county of Lancaster, the 10th day of February 1634.

Who upon oath informeth, being examined concerning the great meeting of the witches of Pendle, saith that upon All Saint's day last past he, this informer, being with one Henry Parker, a near-door neighbour to him in Wheatley Lane, desired the said Parker to give him leave to gather some bullace, which he did. In gathering whereof he saw two greyhounds, *viz* a black and a brown. One came running over the next field towards him; he verily thinking the one of them to be Master Nutter's, and the other to be Master Robinson's, the said gentlemen then having such like. And saith, the said greyhounds came to him and fawned on him, they having about their necks either of them a collar unto each of which was tied a string, which collars (as this informer affirmeth) did shine like gold. And he thinking that some either of Master Nutter's or Master Robinson's family should have followed them, yet seeing nobody to follow them, he took the same greyhounds thinking to course with them.

And presently a hare did rise very near before him, at the sight whereof he cried 'Loo, loo, loo' but the dogs would not run. Whereupon he, being very angry, took them and with the strings that were about their collars tied them to a little bush at the next hedge, and with a switch that he had in his hand he beat them. And instead of the black greyhound one Dickinson's wife stood up, a neighbour whom this informer knoweth, and instead of the brown one, a little boy, whom this informer knoweth not. At which sight this informer, being afraid, endeavoured to run away. But being stayed by the woman (*viz.* by Dickinson's wife), she put her hand into her pocket and pulled forth a piece of silver much like to a fair shilling and offered to give him it to hold his tongue and not to tell, which he refused saying 'Nay, thou art a witch!' Whereupon, she put her hand into her pocket again and pulled out a thing like unto a bridle that jingled, which she put on the little boy's head; which said boy stood up in the likeness of a white horse and in the brown greyhound's stead.

Then immediately Dickinson's wife took this informer before her upon the said horse and carried him to a new house called Hoarstones being about a quarter of a mile off. Whither, when they were come, there were diverse persons about the door, and he saw diverse others riding on horses of several colours towards the said house, who tied their horses to a hedge near to the said house. Which persons went into the said house, to the number of three-score or thereabouts, as this informer thinketh, where they had a fire and meat roasting in the said house. Whereof a young woman, whom this informer knoweth not, gave him flesh and bread upon a trencher and drink in a glass, which after the first taste he refused and would have no more but said it was naught.

And presently after, seeing diverse of the said company going into a barn near adjoining, he followed after them and there he saw six of them kneeling and pulling, all six of them, six several ropes which were fastened or tied to the top of the barn. Presently after which pulling there came into this informer's sight flesh smoking, butter in lumps, and milk, as it were flying from the said ropes. All which fell into basins which were placed under the said ropes. And after that these six had done, there came other six which did so likewise. And during all the time of their several pulling they made such ugly faces as scared this informer, so that he was glad to run out and steal homewards. Who, immediately finding they wanted one that was in their company, some of them ran after him near to a place in a highway called Boggard Hole, where he (this informer) meet two horsemen, at the sight whereof the said persons left off following him. But the foremost of those persons that followed him he knew to be one Loind's wife, which said wife together with one Dickinson's wife and one Janet Davies he hath seen since at several times times in a croft or close adjoining to his father's house, which put him in great fear.

And further, this informer saith, upon Thursday after New Year's Day last past, he saw the said Loind's wife sitting upon a cross-piece of wood being within the chimney of his father's dwelling house and he, calling to her, said 'Come down thou, Loind's wife!' And immediately the said Loind's wife went up out of his sight. And further this informer saith that after he was come from the company aforesaid to his father's house, being towards evening, his father bade him go and fetch home two cows to seal ['fasten in their stalls' OED seal $v.^2$]. And in the way, in a field called the Ellers, he chanced to hap upon a boy who began to quarrel with him, and they fought together till the informer had his ears and face made up very bloody by fighting, and looking down he saw the boy had a cloven foot. At which sight he, being greatly affrighted, came away from him to seek the cows. And in the way he saw a light, like to a lantern, towards which he made haste, supposing it to be carried by some of Master Robinson's people. But when he came to the place he only found a woman standing on a bridge, whom when he saw he knew her to be Loind's wife. And, knowing her, he turned back again and immediately he met with the aforesaid boy from whom he offered to run, which boy gave him a blow on the back that made him to cry.

And further this informer saith that when he was in the barn he saw three women take six pictures from off the beam, in which pictures were many thorns or such-like things sticked in them. And that Loind's wife took one of the pictures down, but the other two women that took down the rest he knoweth not. And being further asked what persons were at the aforesaid meeting, he nominated these persons following, *viz.* Dickinson's wife, Henry Priestley's wife and his lad, Alice Hargreave (widow), Janet Davies, William Davies, and the wife of Henry Facks and her sons John and Miles, the wife of Dennery's, James Hargreave of Marstead, Loind's wife, one James's wife, Saunders's wife and Saunders himself *sicut credit*, one Lawrence's wife, one Saunder Pinn's wife of Barraford, one Holgate and his wife of Leonards of the West Close.

ACTVS, I. SCENA, I.

Enter Master Arthur, *Mr.* Shakstone, *Mr.* Bantam :
(*as from hunting.*)

Arthur.

As ever sport of expectation,
Thus crost in th' height.
    Shak. Tush these are accidents, all game is
    Arth. So you may call them   (subject to,
Chances, or crosses, or what else you please,
But for my part, Ile hold them prodigies,
As things transcending Nature.
    Bantam. O you speake this,
Because a Hare hath crost you.
    Arth. A Hare ? a Witch, or rather a Divell I think.
For tell me Gentlemen, was't possible
In such a faire course, and no covert neere,
We in pursuit, and she in constant view,
Our eyes not wandring but all bent that way,
The Dogs in chase, she ready to be ceas'd,
And at the instant, when I durst have layd
My life to gage, my Dog had pincht her, then
To vanish into nothing!
    Shak. Somewhat strange, but not as you inforce it,
    Arth. Make it plaine
That I am in an error, sure I am
That I about me have no borrow'd eyes.
They are mine owne, and Matches.
    Bant. She might find some Muse as then not visible to us,
And escape that way.
    Shak. Perhaps some Foxe had earth'd there,

B   And

Facsimile of *The Late Lancashire Witches* (London, 1634) fol.Bi.
Reproduced by kind permission of the British Library (C.34.C.54).